Gregory Ghosts: Haunting Irishness

Reimagining Ireland
VOL. 147

Edited by Dr Eamon Maher
Technological University Dublin – Tallaght Campus

Kevin P. Reilly

Gregory Ghosts: Haunting Irishness

PETER LANG

Oxford · Berlin · Bruxelles · Chennai · Lausanne · New York

Bibliographic Information published by the Deutsche Nationalbibliothek
The Deutsche Nationalbibliothek lists this publication in the Deutsche Nationalbibliografie; detailed bibliographic data is available online at http://dnb.d-nb.de.

A catalogue record for this book is available from the British Library.

Library of Congress Cataloging-in-Publication Data

Names: Reilly, Kevin (Literary scholar) author
Title: Gregory ghosts: haunting Irishness / Kevin Reilly.
Description: Oxford; New York: Peter Lang, 2026. | Series: Reimagining Ireland, 16629094; vol 147 | Includes bibliographical references.
Identifiers: LCCN 2025045153 (print) | LCCN 2025045154 (ebook) | ISBN 9781803747422 paperback | ISBN 9781803747439 pdf | ISBN 9781803747446 epub
Subjects: LCSH: English literature--Irish authors--History and criticism | English literature--19th century--History and criticism | English literature--20th century--History and criticism | Gregory, Lady, 1852-1932--Family | Literature and society--Ireland--History | National characteristics, Irish, in literature | Ireland--In literature | LCGFT: Creative nonfiction | Monologues (Drama) | Literary criticism
Classification: LCC PR8750 .R45 2026 (print) | LCC PR8750 (ebook) | DDC 820.9/9415--dc23/eng/20260121
LC record available at https://lccn.loc.gov/2025045153
LC ebook record available at https://lccn.loc.gov/2025045154

Cover image: Lady Gregory on a bench at Coole Park. Courtesy of Colin Smythe.
Cover design by Peter Lang Group AG

ISSN 1662-9094
ISBN 978-1-80374-742-2 (Print)
ISBN 978-1-80374-743-9 (ePDF)
ISBN 978-1-80374-744-6 (ePUB)
DOI 10.3726/ b23107

© 2026 Peter Lang Group AG, Lausanne (Switzerland)
Published by Peter Lang Ltd, Oxford (United Kingdom)

info@peterlang.com

Kevin P. Reilly has asserted his right under the Copyright, Designs and Patents Act, 1988, to be identified as Author of this Work.

All rights reserved.
All parts of this publication are protected by copyright.
Any utilization outside the strict limits of the copyright law, without the permission of the publisher, is forbidden and liable to prosecution. This applies in particular to reproductions, translations, microfilming, and storage and processing in electronic retrieval systems.

This publication has been peer reviewed.

www.peterlang.com

Table of Contents

Figures vii
Preface ix
Acknowledgements xiii
Introduction xv

CHAPTER 1
Lady Augusta Gregory *Ave* 1852–1932 1

CHAPTER 2
Sir William Gregory 1816–1892 13

CHAPTER 3
Wilfrid Scawen Blunt 1840–1922 23

CHAPTER 4
John Quinn 1870–1924 35

CHAPTER 5
William Butler Yeats 1865–1939 45

CHAPTER 6
Maud Gonne 1866–1953 55

CHAPTER 7
Hugh Lane 1875–1915 69

CHAPTER 8
Maire Nic Shiubhlaigh (Mary Elizabeth Walker) 1883–1958 79

CHAPTER 9
Robert Gregory 1881–1918 91

CONTENTS

CHAPTER 10
Lady Augusta Gregory *Vale* 1852–1932 105

Sources 115

List of Figures

Figure 1. Lady Gregory as a young woman. Courtesy of Colin Smythe xx

Figure 2. Sir William Gregory. Courtesy of Colin Smythe 12

Figure 3. Wilfrid Scawen Blunt. Courtesy of Colin Smythe 22

Figure 4. John Quinn. Public Domain, National Portrait Gallery, Smithsonian Institution; painted by John Butler Yeats 34

Figure 5. William Butler Yeats. Public Domain, Chicago Daily News Collection, Chicago History Museum 44

Figure 6. Maud Gonne. Courtesy of Colin Smythe 54

Figure 7. Hugh Lane. Courtesy of Colin Smythe 68

Figure 8. Maire Nic Shiubhlaigh. Courtesy of the Abbey Theatre Archive 78

Figure 9. Robert Gregory. Courtesy of Colin Smythe 90

Figure 10. Lady Gregory later in life. Courtesy of Colin Smythe 104

Preface

This is a ghost story. It's about ghosts looking back over their lives – and sometimes forward beyond them – to try to make sense of them, their times and one another.

Each is the ghost of a real person, an Irish or Irish-American person involved in the Irish Literary Renaissance of the late nineteenth and early twentieth centuries. These nine were entwined with one another too, as friends, frenemies, artistic collaborators, lovers, family members and political actors straddling an Irish Sea of contention and connection between Ireland and England. Their ghostly status gives them rein to muse more freely and believe they see things more clearly than they would have been able to during life.

Theirs were all turbulent lives played out on the western edge of Europe at a time of great change that shaped the course of the twentieth century, and that reverberates still in the twenty-first. Ireland was a kind of European third-world colony when it gained qualified independence from England in 1922 after 800 years of domination. That independence was won between two world wars in a long era of modern, violent conflict among nations, religions and ethnicities. In Ireland's case, the conflict was between Ireland and England, Catholics and Protestants, Celts and Anglo-Saxons. It was a precursor to other twentieth-century uprisings by indigenous nationalist movements against empires and colonisers.

Often accompanying and impelling such movements were rejuvenations of the faded or repressed cultural inheritances of peoples occupied both militarily and psychologically. The Irish Literary Renaissance was such a reclaiming. It led up to and continued beyond the Irish Rising of Easter Monday, 1916. As William Butler Yeats famously wondered in his poem, 'Man and the Echo': 'Did that play of mine send out/Certain men the English shot?' Yeats's mentor, writing partner and friend, Lady Augusta Gregory, was as responsible as anyone for bringing forward Irish folklore, mythologies and heroic tales into a modern world that would use them for its own liberating purposes.

Lady Gregory (1852–1932) is the main character in this book. Thus, its ghosts are 'Gregory Ghosts'. As playwright, as a founder of the Irish Literary Theatre and as a director of the Abbey Theatre, she was artist, businesswoman, inspiration to other artists and imperious conductor of the tumultuous – and very male – Irish Renaissance 'orchestra'. She was, too, an English lady, running her grand estate in County Galway, Coole Park, as a widow, with tender dedication to the land and its tenants, as well as an iron will she imposed on both.

She was an inveterate memoirist and an adept organiser of American tours for her Abbey Theatre company. She adroitly negotiated between Protestants and Catholics, Irish unionists and Irish rebels, Irish Free-Staters and Irish Republicans, clergy and laypeople, and Dublin and London galleries in defending the integrity of Irish art. So, we might say today, perhaps to this proper Victorian woman's horror, that she was a proto-feminist. She demonstrated her superior abilities in a range of realms, prefiguring the rise of women in so many of them from which they had been excluded. The defining political, social and cultural structures in which she did so were being reinvented throughout her long lifetime.

Ireland was becoming an independent nation, but only after enduring the triple agonies of the failed 1916 uprising, the Anglo-Irish War (1919–21) and, right on its heels, the Irish Civil War (1922–3). Her Anglo-Irish Protestant Ascendancy tribe was losing power and influence, most strikingly embodied by their eventual displacement from the grand country houses and estates that were the most visible icons of their authority and wealth. Aristocracies and monarchies everywhere were waning, the middle class and democracy waxing.

The most prominent Irish writers that her Irish Revival would enable in poetry, fiction and drama – Yeats, Joyce and Beckett, respectively – were in their very different ways middle-class iconoclasts, thoroughly familiar with tradition but turning it on its head for modernist effect. Then there was the unthinkable trauma of World War I, leaving some forty million wounded and dead. It would claim her only child, Robert, in a plane crash in Italy. The world in which she died in 1932 was hardly the one she had been born into in 1852. Somehow, she managed to evolve with it all.

I have been reading Irish literature since well before I wrote my doctoral dissertation about Irish literary autobiography more than forty years ago. Lady Augusta Gregory remains, for me, a unique, unlikely mover in the Irish tradition, a bundle of the contradictions mentioned above, a woman who brought them together to appropriate the Irish past for herself and use it to propel Ireland into a new and different future. In that sense, her spirit has haunted the richly contentious, innovative and lively Irish literary landscape since her death, and haunts it still. She was a ghostly presence in her own time as well in that she served as a sort of ghostwriter for her male colleagues, doing much work behind the scenes for which she got little or no credit.

The contemporary American writer Barbara Kingsolver has said, 'The alchemy of literature is in its translation of global-scale themes – like, let's say, the disposition of social collapse – into the intimate language of human experience'. Lady Gregory was indispensable in helping her fellow writers practice that alchemy in their fraught Irish moment. The interior monologue is the most intimate literary distillation of human experience. Each character in this book has one of her or his own.

They include her much older, mutton-chopped husband, Sir William Gregory; their son, Robert; the charming, dilettantish womaniser, Wilfrid Scawen Blunt, with whom she had an affair; Yeats, her mentee and friend, whose prodigious talents blossomed with her careful cultivation of them; and Maire Nic Shiubhlaigh, the young Abbey Theatre actress and nationalist, at once sceptical of the grand lady's airs and intentions and admiring of her strength and determination. Others in the Gregory circle also appear. Lady Gregory gets two monologues, as the originator and the closer of this ghost story.

These monologues interact with each other, making them at once more intimate and more public. The characters are talking from beyond the grave with one another, if obliquely, if not directly to one another. These interactions are charged with an enhanced hindsight, and foresight, appropriate to their ghostly personae.

My method in writing the book was appropriate to its unusual genre. I, of course, read drama, poetry, memoirs, letters, autobiographies, biographies, essays and histories written by and about the characters. I wrote each chapter with as many of these pertaining to the character speaking in the chapter as available to me on and around my desk. I would refer to these sources as I wrote, moving among them as the chapter took shape, drawing ideas from them as well as words spoken or written by the characters themselves.

I have not put these ideas and words in quotation marks with footnotes or endnotes. Introducing such scholarly apparatus would have disrupted the flow of these interior monologues, the sense that the ghostly speakers are giving us an unfettered piece of their minds. The book is not literary criticism, or academic history, or biography, but an imaginative recreation of the characters' personalities and views, informed by scholarship and their own writing.

After the final chapter, I have provided in a 'Sources' section a thorough description of the publications and collections I relied on in writing each chapter. There, readers can follow up as they wish on the primary and secondary sources that inform each chapter and that delineate the lives of the real people represented here by their chatty ghosts.

Just what kind of a ghost story is this, after all that? I would say it is one sung by a chorus of complementary and competing Irish voices, preternaturally informed in their afterlives. I have not 'made up' any facts about these characters. What they think about the facts reflects very much what they themselves have written and what credible others have written about them. Based on these accounts, I have shaped what I'll call their 'cast of mind' to project how I believe they might see themselves and others if they knew something of what was to come after their deaths.

The book is thus a literary version of a carefully curated portrait gallery. Reading it is similar to the experience of a visitor to an art gallery who might view a number of paintings or photographs of individuals of the same place, time and culture, and think about how the subjects might interpret their own lives today in light of what those lives together set in motion.

In 'The Municipal Gallery Revisited', Yeats urges his readers to

> come to this hallowed place
> Where my friends' portraits hang and look thereon;
> Ireland's history in their lineaments trace;
> Think where man's glory most begins and ends
> And say my glory was I had such friends.

My hope for my readers is that they will find this collection of ghostly portraits and voices, dominated by the presence of an Irishwoman of fascinating facets and counterpoints, worth the visit.

Acknowledgements

Let me start at the beginning. All four of my grandparents were immigrants from Ireland, admitted through Ellis Island to their new American lives in New York City. My father, John Reilly, an avid reader himself, led me into the thicket of the Irish written word. My mother, Margaret Cunningham Reilly, was always supportive of my literary interests, if occasionally concerned that I was reading dirty books by James Joyce. I was encouraged by all the members of my large Irish family to learn about and celebrate the songs of my tribe as they appear in poetry and prose.

Professor Edward Cronin of the University of Notre Dame introduced me as an undergraduate to the glories and difficulties of Joyce. He led an independent study seminar where we read, out loud, a few pages of *Finnegans Wake* each week, and tried to make sound sense of it all. Joyce became my expansive gateway to the Irish literary canon, ancient to modern. Professor Chester Anderson, the University of Minnesota's renowned Joyce scholar, took me under his wing as a graduate student. I worked with him as a teaching assistant in his Joyce course. His broad and deep knowledge of Irish literature I set myself to try to emulate. His engaged mentorship throughout my graduate student years culminated in his chairing the faculty committee overseeing my dissertation on Irish literary autobiography, and then urging me to produce scholarly articles drawn from it. Without that immersion in Irish life writing, this book would not have been possible.

My colleague at the University of Wisconsin-Madison and eminent Irish historian, Professor James Donnelly, Jr, recruited me to the board of directors of the Irish American Cultural Institute, and generously offered to read the book manuscript. He improved it with his sharp editorial eye. He was kind enough to contribute the Introduction to the book.

ACKNOWLEDGEMENTS

Catherine Owers got the manuscript into splendid submission shape for Peter Lang with care and competence. Anthony Mason of Peter Lang has been encouraging and understanding from the time he first read the book proposal.

I was lucky to have my good friend from graduate school days, Tom Grady, as my book whisperer. Tom has worked as an editor, editorial director and publisher for such companies as Harper San Francisco and Ave Maria Press. He has also been a literary agent. Tom lent me the benefit throughout of his vast knowledge about making and publishing books, thereby helping to keep me putting one authorial foot in front of the other.

My wife Kate was the first reader of the drafts of book chapters. She made good suggestions for clarifying my telling of the speakers' stories for readers not steeped in Irish culture and history. She also graciously tolerated the decade-long uproarious clutter of books by and about Lady Gregory and friends in my small home study. She will not know what to do with the newly liberated space, or me, now that this book is finished. Her love and support, and that of our three children, Liam, Adriana and Darvin, motivated me to see the project through.

Introduction

This ingenious, absorbing and lively new book employs a novel technique to explore the human relationships and personal connections that created and propelled the Irish Literary Revival of the late nineteenth and early twentieth centuries. It foregrounds the lives of nine distinct and important persons who played leading roles in this renaissance, with Lady Augusta Gregory and William Butler Yeats occupying what might be called the foremost positions in this linked collection of ghostly figures. Its members are cast as ghosts to enable each of them not only to look back over their lives but also to gaze into the future in efforts to make sense of their existence, their times, and their contemporaries.

The passage of land legislation after 1880 in response to agrarian violence and furious agitation by tenants and their political supporters was gravely undermining the economic, political and cultural domination of members of the Anglo-Irish and Protestant Ascendancy. The flurry of new land laws was shattering the grip of the traditional landowning class, many of whom resided in Britain for most or even all of the year. The wiser members of the landed Ascendancy could see the writing on the wall. In response those aristocrats or gentry unsympathetic or loosely attached to the cause of British imperialism – a growing minority – gravitated toward or even firmly embraced the cause of Irish nationalism and especially Irish cultural nationalism.

At the turn of the century Irish cultural nationalism assumed numerous guises, but among its most distinctive forms were the Irish Literary Revival and the Irish Dramatic Movement. Among organisations at the head of this rejuvenation were members of the Irish National Literary Society (INLS), formally inaugurated in Dublin in mid-August 1892, following less than a year after the establishment of its English progenitor at the London home of William Butler Yeats. There was considerable overlap in membership and aims between these two bodies. Thus, the movers behind the launching of the INLS were Yeats again and Douglas Hyde, but this time aided by Lady Augusta Gregory and Edward Martyn. Both organisations were dedicated to achieving the revival and preservation of lapsed Irish customs and to reversing foreign influences (read English/British) in Irish culture through the development of Anglo-Irish literature. (Other bodies founded soon afterward sought different objectives, seeking to create or revive an Irish literature that would find its voice in the Gaelic language. Their leaders and followers became known as Irish–Irelanders.)

Within a half-dozen years Yeats, Lady Gregory, and Martyn set out on a new course with the founding of the Irish Literary Theatre (ILT) in 1898. Its first productions were staged early in May of that year, when on successive nights at the Ancient Concert Rooms in Dublin its founders presented Yeats's *Countess Cathleen* and Martyn's *The Heather Field*. The leaders and playwrights of this new departure soon showed considerable enthusiasm for theatrical works in the Irish language and about peasant culture, as first demonstrated by the staging of Douglas Hyde's *Casadh an tSúgán* (The Twisting of the Rope) at Dublin's Gaiety Theatre in October 1901.

In company with the National Dramatic Company of the Fay brothers (Frank and Willy), the ILT launched the Irish National Theatre Society in 1903. Among its first productions was John Millington Synge's rousing play *In the Shadow of the Glen*, first performed in October of that year in Dublin's Molesworth Hall. This theatrical success was followed shortly thereafter in February 1904 by his *Riders to the Sea* in the same venue. Though certain of Synge's plays elicited strong negative reactions from political nationalists, Irish–Irelanders and Catholic moralists, especially *The Playboy of the Western World* at the end of January 1907, their literary merits were unquestionable and have stood the test of time.

From the ILT the now famous (indeed world-renowned) Abbey Theatre emerged beginning in 1904 and came to feature a distinct, highly productive and immensely influential school of playwrights and actors, of whom Lady Gregory and Yeats were among the most prolific dramatists along with Synge. In fact the Abbey opened on 27 December of that year with *On Baile's Strand* by Yeats and *Spreading the News* by Lady Gregory, using a building in Abbey Street in Dublin, formerly the Mechanics' Institute, bought and adapted by Miss A. E. F. (Annie) Horniman and given to the National Theatre Society. Horniman also heavily subsidised the Abbey Theatre for six years.

The respective and often mutual achievements and contributions of the Gregory ghosts in relation to the Irish dramatic movement were highly impressive or at least very useful. In the quarter century between 1901 and 1928, Lady Gregory alone authored or co-authored more than forty plays, most of which came to life on the Abbey stage. Her many translations and adaptations entirely apart, her plays engaged in novel ways with the daily lives, myths and tribulations of the peasantry who were for the most part tenants on her estate of Coole Park near Gort in County Galway; she also learned much about these distinctive features of Irish popular culture from the inmates of the local poor-law workhouse. Her plays generally adopted 'the heightened language and exaggerated poetry based on the idiom' familiar to her from her habit of visiting her own tenants' humble dwellings – an idiom sometimes dubbed Hiberno-English.

Lady Gregory's friendship with Yeats began in 1896, and thereafter he often visited her at Coole Park (as did other literary titans). The two closely collaborated in writing plays, in promoting the work of the Abbey Theatre, and in encouraging other dramatists associated with the Abbey, most notably Synge, whom Yeats in particular had encouraged to further his talents by immersing himself in the experiences of the people of the Aran Islands. From Synge's immersion was to spring an arresting series of plays capturing and interpreting the lives and customs of these islanders. Among these dramas, in addition to the three already mentioned, were *The Well of the Saints* (1905) and *The Tinkers Wedding* (1908), his last before his death from cancer in 1909.

Other Gregory ghosts played lesser (if still important) roles than Synge, Yeats and Lady Gregory. Five of them might be mentioned very briefly. One was her husband William, whom she married at twenty-seven, even though he was sixty-three. He had spent his career as a parliamentary politician and governor of Ceylon. Another was her lover Wilfred Scawen Blunt, the diplomat, author, anti-imperialist and serial philanderer whose diaries were published long after their affair (in 1919–20), but with a foreword by Lady Gregory herself. A third was Maud Gonne, the agrarian militant, anti-imperialist, arch-republican and suffragette. This last cause prompted her to co-found the nationalist organisation Inghinidhe na hÉireann (Daughters of Ireland) at Easter 1900. Two years later, Gonne played the leading role in Yeats's play *Cathleen ní Houlihan*. She was widely admired as a woman of great beauty, and Yeats was smitten with her and proposed marriage on several occasions – all unsuccessful.

A fourth was Maire Nic Shuiblaigh (Mary Elizabeth Walker), whose youth, middle-class background and Catholic nationalist upbringing at first distanced her from the much older, aristocratic and Protestant Lady Gregory, but whose relationship with her later warmed up, especially in admiration for Augusta's defiant stance in response to rioters against Synge's *Playboy* during the Abbey's U.S. tour of 1911–2. A fifth was the New Yorker and lawyer John Quinn, whose links with the chief figures in the Irish Literary Renaissance were strong. His professional skills were of great use to the Abbey players during their American tour of 1912–3 after they encountered popular rejection and legal troubles over Synge's *Playboy of the Western World*.

In the same category of lesser importance (yet still very significant) was the sixth personality – Sir Hugh Lane, the famous Cork-born art collector and dealer, who amassed a world-class art collection. Among his resounding contributions to the visual arts in Ireland, the best known is his founding of Dublin's Municipal Gallery of Modern Art in January 1908 (now the Hugh Lane Gallery); it is the first known public gallery of modern art in the world. He was the nephew of Lady Gregory, who (along with others) became his champion after the Dublin Corporation on grounds of cost declined in 1912 to build a national gallery *specifically for modern art* that would display Lane's invaluable collection featuring especially the French Impressionists. While returning to England from America, he drowned on the *Lusitania* on 7 May 1915.

At the time of Lane's death, he had been director of the National Gallery of Ireland for fourteen months. Though Lane had first meant to gift almost forty of his Impressionist paintings to this gallery, he despaired of sufficient official Irish support and bequeathed these paintings to the National Gallery in London. But he changed his mind in favour of Dublin shortly before his death, leaving unsigned a new codicil of his will to this effect, and consequently his intentions were frustrated, with these paintings going instead to the National Gallery in London. This omission signalled the start of bitter controversy and litigation in which Lady Gregory and her allies became his champions (Friends of the National Gallery of Ireland) in a decades-long campaign to secure these artworks for the Dublin institution.

The author of this excellent book skilfully examines and elucidates the many layers of interconnection between and among the Gregory ghosts and charts their life stories in a highly compelling manner that this introduction only begins to suggest. In sum, Kevin P. Reilly makes a fresh, vibrant and fascinating contribution to the scholarly and popular literature on the Irish dramatic movement and the wider Irish Literary Renaissance.

James S. Donnelly, Jr
Professor Emeritus of History, University of Wisconsin-Madison
Chairman, Board of Directors, Irish American Cultural Institute

Figure 1. Lady Gregory as a young woman. Courtesy of Colin Smythe.

CHAPTER 1

Lady Augusta Gregory *Ave* 1852–1932

See the Preface for an overview of Lady Gregory's life and times.

Men. Irish men. Anglo-Irish men worse still. They have all troubled this woman's heart and occupied her mind as they live their careless and careful lives.

Father, husband, lover, son, brother, artist, rabble, cottier, colleague, collaborator, rebel, corpse. They create and they destroy with a heedless freedom that stymies women. But the women would be stymied, so many of them. Not worth talking to. No nose for politics and a timid taste in art.

I wonder if my unease with women goes back to my mother, 'The Mistress', as I always called her. Imagine – she told me as a child not to think of myself as the equal of my sisters, all tall and handsome. Then insinuating my husband, Sir William, of her generation, had married me as a compliment to her, fussing with that Maltese shawl he had given her, and then bestowing it on me as a reminder.

Well, I understand a woman's place in the Victorian empire. I have played in that place while directing the play from the wings. If the mask becomes the man, the mask of the Abbey Theatre has been a becoming one for me, and behind it I have changed the face of Ireland and fashioned my own worldly demeanour. Always the maternal lady of Coole Park, but also a lordly actor strutting the world stage, despite and around and in the midst of those madly acting men.

With my ghostly gaze, now I see their past and their future. What was it James Joyce's Anna Livia Plurabelle felt about them as the life poured out of her? 'And I am loathing their little warm tricks. And loathing their mean cosy turns. And all the greedy gushes out through their small souls. And all the lazy leaks down over their brash bodies'. He was a conceited, drunken wild one, Joyce was, and

CHAPTER 1

a talent too big and new for little Ireland, even all of Europe, to contain. Only he could proclaim with unparalleled braggadocio: 'If *Ulysses* is unfit to read, life is unfit to live'. So he was right.

His apostle Flann O'Brien was a wild one too. Still, O'Brien's notion about the man and his bicycle amuses me. One of his characters spent so much time riding his bicycle around Dublin that when they went to execute him, they had to hang the bicycle, because there was more of the man in the bicycle than there was in himself. What did Mr Beckett call it – the 'bisexycle'?

Funny. I've always felt myself a binary person. Was there more of me in the Anglo or the Irish? Had I more of a feminine or masculine soul? I was Anglo-Irish landlord and Irish nationalist, faithful wife and guilty mistress, artist and businesswoman, rent collector and philanthropist, traditionalist and modernist, localist and internationalist, conciliator and provocateur. A woman formed by the nineteenth century and unleashed to my own fullness in the twentieth. A speaker of English and a writer of dialect as much Irish as English. I was the only one of the Anglo-Irish Abbey playwrights to study the Irish language seriously, and I retold the ancient Irish myths and sagas the way the Irish people closest to them put them into English. The hyphenated identity is my deep, uncomfortable, enlivening home.

But what is Mother Ireland and her male minions to me after all? Pinching a little truth out of that one without expecting too much clarity has been my life's work and continues to be my ghostly preoccupation.

When my dear, difficult nephew Hugh Lane was harshly criticized after working so hard to bring the best of Ireland's own and other European art to our attention to lift Irish spirits, I thought how is anyone to do anything in this impossible place? But I admit I wrote to my friend John Quinn in America that I did not believe after all that any of us would live away from Ireland if we could – we would miss the quarrelling too much!

Maybe Yeats and I did not quarrel enough over writing our play, *Cathleen Ni Houlihan*. He never gave me the credit I was due. But I did not care. I wanted him to be what he became – our finest poet and the leading man of Irish letters of our time. Selfishly brilliant, but selfless in his pursuit of an Ireland free from its cultural and religious and national shackles.

Class strictures were another thing for Willie. A singer of the aristocratic song, descended from shopkeepers. That awful acerbic moustache of a man George Moore said Yeats looked like an umbrella left behind at a garden party. Yeats understood neither the Irish aristocracy nor the Irish peasantry as I did. He floated over some poetic ground between them. I was born an aristocrat and the peasantry were part of me, on my land and in my house at Coole every day. Their language, their myths, their way of seeing the world, impassioned me to write, to give them a voice I heard with an Englishwoman's ear on one side of my head and an Irish tenant's on the other.

But Yeats I loved because I knew he loved these same things, if he did not understand them in the same way I did. I knew he could develop a powerful Irish voice of his own, with his talent and ambition, his mysticism and hauteur, his outsized love of language, landscape and women. So, I nurtured him, protected him, badgered him and worked alongside him as only a literary Irishwoman of my class could.

His persistent, manipulative paramour, Maud Gonne, said, 'Willie was so silly'. But I was the one who recognised early that it was silly genius. Genius that needed to be pampered, pushed and shaped into seriousness. I've never regretted playing the woman behind the Yeatsian throne, because in that role I enabled him to give the full measure of his gift to Ireland, and through her to the world.

Her. Why do we always imagine Ireland as a woman? America has Uncle Sam, a stringy nanny goat wrapped in his flag tuxedo. But there is Columbia too, a graceful beauty of liberty presiding over New York harbour. Good to have a welcoming, imposing woman there. Mother Russia embraces, shields her endless territories and grieves over her endless suffering. But England is John Bull, all forward-leaning, masculine, big-bellied blunt aggression. An icon of omnivorous Anglo empire that makes Mother Ireland mourn over 800 years of control and contempt.

Bismarck, I was told, thought Europe was divided into two sexes. He saw the female countries – Italy and our own Celtic ones, for example – having a soft, pleasing quality and the charm of a woman, but no capacity for self-government. The male countries needed to take them in hand. John Bull well followed the advice of his German cousin in his dealings with his abused Irish mistress.

By the end of our play *Cathleen Ni Houlihan*, old woman Ireland has transformed into a young queen. But she's a bloody one in either form, demanding that Irish men sacrifice themselves for her. As the doomed Irish rebels from 1916, Pearse and Connolly, agree in Yeats's 'Rose Tree' poem:

> There's nothing but our own red blood
> Can make a right Rose Tree.

Pearse especially, ardent Catholic that he was, believed in the efficacy of blood sacrifice. Just as God the Father somehow needed to sacrifice his only Son to free the world from sin and darkness, so the blood of Irish patriots must be shed to free Mother Ireland from the oppression of John Bull colonialism.

And flow it did, with so many of them stood up against a wall in Kilmainham Jail and shot dead by firing squad. The scholarly, devout schoolmaster Pearse foresaw it as a holy re-enactment of the Romanish ritual of the Mass – bodies and blood – that would nourish Irish freedom on to the glory of an Irish state. It did so, with barrel loads of blood rolling on through an Irish Free State to an Irish Republic – a republic of great glory to some and profound disappointment to others.

Democratic governments are that compromise that pleases no one fully, certainly not the true believers. It is hard to be enthusiastic about balance when you're a patriot. But it is dangerous to be enthusiastic about one-eyed unyieldingness in any government. Didn't our Irish Civil War show us that?

The sacrifice to achieve an independent yet unenthusiastic sharing of power by Irish men and women can seem too great. Before his execution Pearse said he knew the Rising could not succeed, but 'a sacrifice was necessary'. 'Too long a sacrifice makes a stone of the heart', wrote Yeats. He was talking about what the unyielding passion for the freedom of Mother Ireland had done to damage the life of his lover, Maud Gonne. He was thinking too of the lives of Pearse and Connolly and Plunkett and MacDonagh and the other poets, artists and dreamers who took up arms and thereby took on suicide when their words failed to provoke their fellow Irishmen into rebellion.

Has history ever seen a less likely squad of armed revolutionaries? Our own Abbey Theatre actor, Arthur Shields, at first unaware of what was happening around him on the Easter Monday of the Rising, then felt honour bound to join it. But he told his fellow rebels he was to act in an Abbey Theatre matinee, and the commander said he might go and act, and come back and join them afterward.

Dubliners initially were unmoved by the assault on the British Empire – if that's not too grand a thing to call it. Many were unhappy about its disruption of normal life in their capital city. Some, as in all such situations, took advantage of the chaos. A looter was said to have carried out a load from a shop and laid it on the pavement. While she was getting another load somebody carried off the first. When she came back out she flew into a rage and cursed and said wasn't it a terrible country where you couldn't lay a thing down but it would be taken.

The rebels died nobly for such as these, who came to see them as heroes after the hasty justice of official English rifles accommodated their intent on martyrdom. And though their words had not fomented broad Irish support for their violent rebellion, they used them to achieve the purpose they would not live to see fulfilled. Our Abbey playwright turned insurgent Thomas MacDonagh saying: 'Men see in their own day the truth of their own day. So it is still revered the martyr-blood that once was traitor blood'.

Maud Gonne's estranged husband John MacBride, accused of being a drunk and molesting his stepdaughter, summoned the courage to turn down an offered blindfold. He said kindly to his English executioner whose hands were trembling: 'Don't take to heart anything that it is your duty to do as a soldier. I have looked down the barrels of English rifles all my life'.

I myself did not know what to make of them at first. Were they reckless, vainglorious, irresponsible idealists? I think now their reckless idealism is their genius. Pearse's Irish language poem 'Mise Eire' is a summons to defend the honour of the betrayed Old Woman:

I am Ireland
Older than the Hag of Beara.

Great my pride:
I gave birth to brave Cuchulain.

Great my shame:
My own children sold their mother.

They were sure – absolutely sure – that their actions would restore Ireland's pride, redeem her shame, and bring to the lonely Old Woman millions of fervent supporters to renew her soul. Their self-generated, manly tragedy is both compelling and repulsive to me. They had to wrench the beauty of Irish life all out of shape, decimate it, to put it back together in freer form. I claim no clear, settled arithmetic of the gains and losses.

But the loss that came two years later – in 1918 – was sure to crush me, I believed. Its looming had haunted me ever since my dear, lovely son Robert, my only child, had joined the Connaught Rangers in 1915 and then the Royal Flying Corps in 1916, to fight the Germans. I could not help but wonder, pushing it back always in my mind, its always seeping, sneaking forward again, how one would hear, how one would bear the news. Every evening, I had been thankful that no such news had come. Every morning, I had prayed for the safety of my child. When I received a telegram beginning, 'Deeply regret', my heart had seemed to stop before I could take in the other words. But it was only regret from friends at the breaking of some engagement.

When I was handed the later telegram at Coole Park it was addressed to 'Mrs Gregory'. I thought, this is telling of Robert's death, meant for his wife, Margaret. Nevertheless, I looked, and the first words I saw were 'killed in action', and then at the top, 'Deeply regret'. He had died on 23 January 1918. My mind ran wildly to Margaret and the young, innocent children who were in Galway with my sister. How can I tell her? Who will tell her? I tried to stand up but could not.

I felt that I must not cry or think but fix my mind on one thing. Who is in Galway to tell Margaret? Who can go? I cannot go. But go I must. On the

CHAPTER 1

train there was an Englishwoman who made tea for herself, got out her lunch-basket, and invited me to join her. I could but shake my head. How could she not understand she was near so much grief? But I was glad she did not guess. As the train sped along, I felt it was cruel to be going so quickly to break Margaret's heart. I wished the train could go slower. When I arrived at the house, it was agony knowing the journey was at an end. I went to my sister's room and told the maid to send Margaret to me there. I stood there, and she came in. She blurted out at once, 'Is he dead?' Then we sat down on the floor and cried down the rain.

How we longed to have back the ebullient little boy who grew to become a fine painter, a brave soldier, a loving husband and father, a generous landlord. His paintings graced many a gallery. His renderings of our western Ireland landscape with its spare intensity were particularly moving. The scenes he designed and painted for Abbey Theatre performances turned the inside of the theatre into outside Ireland. Boxer, cricketer, horseman, he was a favourite of his friends, his military comrades, and his commanders.

So many of them wrote or talked to me to remind me of his virtues, of which of course I needed no reminding; but they wanted to remember him and be kind to his mother. A newspaper article got it just right in portraying 'a man so much the artist that he was never at pains to seem one, so much a man that the unobservant might never guess he was an artist'. One of our tenants recalled his bravado on the back of a horse:

> It was never the courage failed him. There was a great run across Moneen and they came to a gate, and not one would face it, but Mr Robert. And when he did they all shut their eyes. But he got over safe and sound.

The poor coming to the door all had their memories, one telling me that if he had been a gentleman, Robert could make no more of him. Another saying Robert would give him a whole hand when they saw each other, never an empty one. Still another comforting me with this loveliness: 'Let you rise the trouble off your mind. He loved his wife and he loved his children and he loved his mother, and may God love him for that'.

George Bernard Shaw, as usual, had one of the most interesting things to say. He told me that when he met Robert at his Flying Corps base, with a barely healed case of frostbite on his face from flying in frigid weather, Robert proclaimed that his six months there had been the happiest of his life. An amazing proclamation, thought Shaw, considering the privilege of his life at home. Shaw speculated that to a man with Robert's power of standing up to danger, war must have intensified his life as nothing else could, not even art or love. My mysterious son – the gentle, kind artist with the common touch who enjoyed himself in war, an Irishman in an English quarrel with the middle of the Continent.

Those rumours when he was born that he was not the son of my elderly husband, Sir William. William perhaps stoked the rumours with his obvious discomfort at the prospect of fatherhood, and his surprise and annoyance at the demands the pregnancy made of me, and him. He was torn about whether it would keep him in Ireland through the Fall instead of running off to southern Italy. It didn't. He left me at home at Coole. When he returned to Ireland, Dublin easily drew him away from my bouts of ill health carrying Robert.

William was sixty-three when we wed, and I was twenty-seven. He was a friend of my parents and a neighbour. We had so much in common, even if we were not in love at that time. And by marrying Sir William I could start to establish an identity free of my family, yet stay close to them in a part of the world I did not want to leave. His was a most attractive proposal, and it led to a serene, affectionate, proper life together for twelve years, until his death in 1892. My relationships with Wilfrid Blunt and John Quinn were of a different order.

But back when I got pregnant with Robert, the gossips wanted to believe that the handsome blacksmith who worked for us, Seanin Farrell, was the father. They whispered he had been spirited off to America with the other emigrants after doing his good deed. The Irish are wont to confuse legend with reality, reality with legend. They made a legend of Robert's birth and death, just like the Irish sagas, indeed all countries' myths, do with their heroes. Yet as a student of myth I know well that it is a way of explaining what is most real about people and their relationships. I should stop there musing about Robert's paternity, which finally makes little difference in the grand scheme of things, and go back to his loss and legacy.

In death, the Continent has him now and forever, buried as he is close to where he died in Padua, Italy. The poor, uneducated Catholics at Coole Park were glad to know the place of his interment. One said to me: 'Why wouldn't he be happy, being laid in the holy ground of Padua where St Anthony was a great saint?' In Roman Catholic lore, St Anthony of Padua is painted cradling the infant Jesus in his arms more than any other saint except his mother, Mary. In my religious moments I can hope St Anthony is warmly embracing my only son as Mary did hers.

I never knew that the records of the Royal Flying Corps would show that Robert was shot down in error by an Italian pilot. The waste of it. Despite the eventual Allied victory, I am overwhelmed not only by Robert's loss, but also by the loss of so many young, promising men in my family. Four of my nephews

CHAPTER 1

fell fighting in France. My brother's sons Rudolf, Dudley, Henry and Aubrey Persse. Another nephew, another Dudley Persse, a sailor wounded on a burning ship in the Mediterranean, came home to die. His elder brother, Geoffrey, was killed at Gallipoli.

Nor was the next generation spared. A young great-nephew, Percy Trench, died in a battle beside the Tigris. Hugh Lane, my sister's son, his frail health not allowing him to go into the war, his last public act the splendid promise of 10,000 pounds for the Red Cross, was lost in the sinking of the *Lusitania*.

There were times when I just wanted to kill Germans. But I don't believe that was what drove Robert. For him it was the thrill, the bravery, the acquisition and the demonstration of his skills in the air, the opportunity to lead other men, the ideal of fighting on the side of right. Right is not so easily defined in these matters, though Yeats has Robert think, in his poem 'An Irish Airman Foresees His Death':

> Those that I fight I do not hate,
> Those that I guard I do not love;

Yeats referred to the British colonialists in that second line. For Robert, it might also refer to the rabid Irish nationalists who threatened Coole Park. A tinge of truth in it for any thinking soldier in any war, I would imagine.

And then the combustible Yeats got carried away by his own hatred for the English Black and Tans brutalising the Irish people in the Anglo-Irish War that extended Ireland's misery after the Great War. That pitch-dark poem of his, 'Reprisals', which he had the decency never to publish, bemoans to Robert's ghost the vicious lashing out, last gasp of John Bull England in Ireland, a John Bull who is 'murdering your tenants there'. Addressing Robert as if he were a duped, defiled corpse, detritus of the British military machine, Yeats tells him:

> Then close your ears with dust and lie
> Among the other cheated dead.

The mother in me hates that poem; the artist in me understands the brute power of it. I am just grateful that the poem was withheld from publication until after my death, and Yeats' own for that matter.

Yeats's language could be genuine comfort, too, as in his poem 'Shepherd and Goatherd':

> She goes about her house erect and calm
> Between the pantry and the linen-chest,
> Or else at meadow or at grazing overlooks
> Her labouring men, as though her darling lived
> But for her grandson now;

When my husband died, I did everything in my power to preserve Coole Park for Robert and his eventual family. He was to be the man of the house and the lord of his demesne. So with his death my daughter-in-law, Margaret, became the lady of the house, and I her tenant. She in turn had to sustain it to be overseen by her and Robert's son, Richard, when he came of age.

We women, rich and aristocratic as we may be, were staff to the patriarchy. So it was with property, so it was in the arts. The Irish Rising changed much for me. The women's rising coming after me changed so much more. The riots over the word 'shift' in *The Playboy of the Western World* in my time perversely foreshadowing the later frenzy about women's foundation garments – the burning of the bras! Ha!

I always knew Coole Park would pass from my husband to the succeeding male generations, with whatever part Margaret would assert along the way. Perhaps knowing that is why when the little boy would have a cough or do a sneeze, it was as if the bones had melted within me. I was so careful about every detail of the place because I wanted them to inherit without debt a home of great dignity, tradition, and beauty. I knew every bush and tree on the property. They all bespoke a design to give comfort, pleasure, joy to Coole's residents over generations.

Didn't I press the government to get the trees along Kiltartan Road vested in a rural council, so that the tenants when they purchased land could not cut them down? Often, I would have to be out all day with my workmen or things would go wrong, with the silvers put on stony ridges and the Scotch in the shade and the wrong sized trees everywhere. For there to be a design there has to be a master designer, like God in Heaven. In this case a mistress designer in Coole Park. God help me, I sometimes wondered if I was preserving Coole for the boys, or preserving the boys for Coole, so it would never lack an appreciative Gregory overseer.

But it would. In 1920, most of it was sold off under the Land Acts. In 1921, with Margaret off with the children to a new house in Celbridge, I started renting the house from her. Finally, in 1927, we sold what was left to the Irish Department of Lands and Agriculture, renting back the house and gardens. After I died in 1932, the place was let deteriorate to where the government sold the house to a building contractor for the price of its stone. He demolished it. We had worked for art and a thinking democracy, and then it sometimes seemed we gave in to a mindless democracy. War and the governments it overturns and produces can feel so futile.

I suppose my love for a place like Coole is rooted in my growing up at Roxborough, the estate of my father's people, the Persses. When my father died and my eldest stepbrother became lord of that house, I first felt the tenant. Would

CHAPTER 1

the rest of us have to abandon our lively household, the great plenty, the fireside comfort, the winter shooting parties, the hillsides of Slieve Echtge where I startled the wild deer climbing to look at the shadowy mountain tops of Connemara beyond the shining Atlantic Bay?

As my son's wife inherited what was his property – not mine – at Coole Park, so my stepbrother inherited my father's estate at Roxborough. Sometime soon as the youngest daughter I would need to forego its stables full of horses, its kennels full of sporting dogs, Gordon setters, retrievers, greyhounds; the sawmill with its carpenters and engineers and turners; the gamekeepers and trappers; the long array of labourers coming each morning to their work; the garden so well tilled, so full in September of grapes and melons and peaches and apples, inexhaustible fruit.

My father defended Roxborough in 1821 against a night-time attack by the radical Irish Ribbonmen, who wanted to stop landlords from changing out or evicting the Catholic tenants. When the Great Famine came in the 1840s, my forebearer Persses did little to help their starving tenants. Many died or left for America. As a young girl at Roxborough in the 1850s and 1860s, the calm on the estate allowed me to roam freely over it, drink it in, make it my own. I wonder if that calm was born of quiet, post-Famine despair on the part of those left working the land. As a young woman in the 1880s, with the Land War in full swing, my love of the place was complicated by what I knew of its history and the then sorry state of relations with the landless labourers who toiled there.

Roxborough's sad end came in the Irish Civil War, when it was pillaged and burned by one of the armed factions. When I went back to see the ruins afterwards with my grandniece, the silence of a once bustling home hurt. It was as if the purple of the slopes of the nearby Slieve Echtge mountains had enshrouded it forever in mourning. But there were brightly coloured phloxes protesting all the weeds in the walled garden. I took them for Coole.

The first time I saw Coole Park I was yet a child, when old Mrs Gregory, my husband-to-be's mother, still presided. She showed us a mulberry tree covered with fruit – and did not offer us any. When I was coming back to Coole the summer after my marriage I looked forward to tasting mulberries. But the old tree was dying and had no fruit. The memory of that disappointed longing for mulberries made me vow to give all visiting children, rich or poor, some little thing to eat or take away with them. My grandniece said once as I took her to rummage in the storeroom, 'It is always Christmas in this house'.

I wanted everyone who visited to feel that way, not just the children. I think all my literary friends did. Yeats, Moore, Martyn, Russell, Synge, Shaw, others, but Yeats most of all, relished their time with me (and sometimes even with each other!) at Coole. It was a kind of writers' perpetual Christmas place.

I wanted it to be a warm home and a bubbling cauldron for the best of Irish thought and expression. I struggled to make and keep it that, just as my husband, William, had struggled to hold onto the property during the Land War. I remember when he wrote to Father Shannon, the tenants' champion, so upset about the destruction of his relationship with his tenants. He told the priest we might have to abandon Coole. Later he noticed some of the workers would no longer touch their caps when they came into his presence. The old order was passing, and he was a man of the old order.

Within a month of coming to Coole as his young wife I was pregnant with Robert. Robert would be there as a child and young man, but never as an old man like his father. World War I took Robert, and eventually Irish heedlessness about the nation's cultural heritage doomed my house at Coole Park. But I have striven to be a realist about such things. As Yeats wrote of Robert, 'What made us dream that he could comb grey hair?' I don't know if that line is cruelty or comfort.

Figure 2. Sir William Gregory. Courtesy of Colin Smythe.

CHAPTER 2

Sir William Gregory 1816–1892

Sir William Gregory was Augusta Gregory's much older, grandly mutton-chopped husband. She was his second wife. When they married, he was sixty-three and she was twenty-seven. He died at age seventy-five, leaving Augusta a young widow at thirty-nine. His family arrived in Ireland with Cromwell. His grandfather and namesake was British Under Secretary for Ireland in the early nineteenth century. A gambler addicted to horse racing, it took marriage to his wealthy first wife, Lizzie, to relieve him of debilitating debt. He travelled widely, served two stints in Parliament, and was Governor of British Ceylon from 1872 to 1877. Augusta had the last say on him, editing and publishing his autobiography two years after his death.

She did love me. So I choose to believe. So what if she wanted to escape the family manse at Roxborough and her better-looking sisters and her overbearing brothers and her grand dame of a self-besotted imperious mother by joining me at Coole Park? That last one would drive the most obsequious cur to the door in short order. Does not many a young woman yearn for the spotlight and servants of her own and the selfless devotion of a man who cares only for her, and can provide? Nothing wrong with that. The institution of marriage and the structures of civilised society rely on such feelings for their very existence. How would everything get on if most of the young ladies stayed comfortable at home?

But the bloody miserable biddies and barons did have their field day when they heard I proposed to Augusta. An old mutton-chopped widower needing a household manager and muse, with perhaps a bit of Saturday night excitement thrown in.

I was lonely. My first wife, Lizzie, was different from Augusta. Ten years younger than I when we wed, Lizzie was already a worldly widow. The horses and the wild turf gambling of my youth had left me in financial straits. The wealth she brought to the marriage freed me from every liability. When she came with me after our marriage to take up the Governorship of Ceylon, we had a comfortable private income besides my official salary.

Lizzie loved Ceylon, perhaps most especially the household we established in the mountains at Nuwara Eliya. We designed together an English garden there, with strawberries and roses, and a fine fowl yard yielding eggs and fat poultry. We built our sheep and pig pens, and cleared walks and drives on our land. The most ungainly swamp we transformed into 'Lake Gregory', a relaxing distraction for the eye and ear from the demands of governing. But this exotic happiness was to prove as brief as it was intense.

When we first arrived in Ceylon my frail wife imbibed an atmosphere that seemed to make her strong and almost fat like the plucky chickens of Nuwara Eliya. She loved the Ceylon butterflies and flowers, sketching them with skill and flair. We worked hard and laughed often. My duties as governor and my interests in the beautiful island – its history, culture, geography, languages – had me travelling often. Lizzie took every opportunity to come along.

But damn all I should have said no to her when she wanted to join me on that trip from Kandy to Amuradhapura. She wheedled her way into the entourage, saying she would find so much to draw along the way, and teasing me that I should not abandon her to the natives at Kandy as I trotted off the hero Governor to be royally received in the provinces. Her bout of diarrhoea before we left I see now so sadly was the warning signal I did not heed.

The horrible stomach pains that night on the road, and the stupid, self-important government agent who met us at Amuradhapura. Fancied himself some kind of expert on tropical diseases. Told us he saw no reason for concern. Lizzie would have nothing to do with the native doctor who offered to see her. Perhaps the fatal flaw of those who exercise colonial powers – the conviction that only their own kind in every profession hold the wisdom of the world.

Either she believed that bastard agent or she wanted to keep from me how sick she really felt. So, I left her at Amuradhapura with her artist friend Constance Cummings, and went on with my official mission. A day later her condition had deteriorated enough that she decided to return to Kandy. Yet emblematic of the generosity of her nature, she stopped for two days on the way to allow Miss Cummings to sketch. Her love of art and regard for a friend prolonged what must have been a tortuous last journey. When Lizzie could stand it no more, her party completed the last 75 kilometres to Kandy in a single day.

They summoned me back from my tour at Kuranegala, and I called the chief medical man up from Colombo to Kandy to attend to her. Dysentery, they said. Serious, but not critical. Within a few days she was dead at age forty-seven.

I think she knew how ill she was in those final days. I held her hand and we sang hymns. Having lived a God-fearing life, she seemed not to fear death so much as leaving me alone.

I ordered a tomb for her from England and wanted nothing so much as to crawl into it myself with her there in Kandy. Polished red granite it was, with the Ceylonese flowers she cherished embracing its base. Her death was the greatest sorrow of my life. We were married but a year and a half before the good Lord saw fit to reclaim her. Happiness dangled so alluringly like the warm lushness of Ceylon before a tropical storm, then violently blown away. Perhaps the follies and iniquities of my early years, so consumed by wagers and wastefulness, justified this sundering. I became for a time half of something that no longer existed, the Governor's house in Colombo a deserted, mournful prison for a half-life.

I have been a man of the broad world, of the many places the British Empire and my wealth it helped amass – much from dear Lizzie's estate – have allowed me to come to know. Lizzie rests on the faraway island of Ceylon. The only child I had with Augusta, the only child I had in the world, Robert, killed in the Great War after I died, was to find an Italian resting place in Padua. My first and last true loves, scattered finally across the globe, far from Ireland and Coole Park.

The empire to which I have always pledged my loyalty has made us a vagabond family. English, Irish, Ceylonese, Italian. It would take Augusta's talents – her peasant plays and Irish mythological tales, her own autobiography and her editing of mine (is that a proper thing for a wife to do to her husband, I wonder), her managing the Abbey Theatre – to put the Gregory name at the centre of a worldly Irishness. She magically mixed the coloniser with the colonised, the local with the international, at last making all the Gregorys, who arrived in Ireland with Cromwell, Irish citizens of the wide world.

Centuries it took to get us there. At first it was the Gregorys as the hated settlers of the Cromwell conquest. We were seen as English overloads sent to live on top of a Celtic powder keg of mad indignation, and muffle the sound of its occasional explosions from English ears with our fortunes and our very bodies. The grandfather with my name, William Gregory, British Under Secretary for Ireland in the early nineteenth century, was a man up to the task. Having survived the rebellion of the United Irishmen in 1798, he knew the best form of government for Ireland was a benevolent despotism.

He was sensitive to the suffering of the poor Catholics who worked the land, writing that it was 'quite impossible for any man with commonsense and common feelings not to see and to bitterly deplore the lamentable poverty of the Irish peasants, and none but a Brute or an Absentee would refuse his money, his labour and his time to promote any rational system for their amelioration'. But he detested and feared their ferocious anti-English sentiment, organised in secret agrarian societies that preyed cruelly on the landlords, as well as any of their own kind who dared to collaborate with the ruling class. He wanted the inadequate law enforcement system in Ireland strengthened, with 'severe' examples made of those who ran afoul of it.

The Catholic Church was the constant, sustained threat to settled law and order in Ireland. The Under Secretary would thwart its plots for Papist power whenever they came to light. He supported the Protestant Crusade of the 1820s to enrol the children of the Catholic peasantry in Protestant Bible Schools. He wanted Irish Catholicism kept down, lest Ireland be lost – as eventually it was. When Daniel O'Connell arose as the fiery, articulate leader for Catholic emancipation, my grandfather and he clashed immediately.

Then gradually, most gradually, almost without our noticing, an Irish identity crept upon us. The gradualness was paradoxically like the suddenness of getting old. Suddenly, it seems, your face is creviced, your hands splotchy and easily bruised, your remaining hair a ghost of itself in volume and colour. You doze after dinner by the fire more quickly but less soundly. How in the name of God did it come on you, this age or this Irishness? The Irishness seems to me now as inevitable as ageing, both processes of unavoidable embrace, profoundly altering identity without making a wholly different man.

I have been affected by many things on my stumbling, half-resisted journey to Irishness in my earthly life and my ghostly life – my love of the rough western Ireland landscape, its cultivation in Coole Park, the sweet temperament of our tenants with their fairy stories and grand myths, the way Augusta raised these up into literature. But the person who best caught my attention about the pathetic polity of Ireland, after my liberal-leaning O'Hara mother, was Daniel O'Connell.

'The Liberator', 'The Emancipator', the great champion of Catholic civil rights and the repeal of the Union with England. That massive figure with darkened face scornful and rancorous in parliamentary debate, vengefully prophesying Irish rebellion and with gloomy smiles exulting in the troubles of England. How he loved his house at Darrynane in County Kerry. When I went up to Parliament, he would tell me of the Atlantic thundering on its stolid cliffs, the sea in all its moods, the music of his beagles, and his home happiness. The English and most of the Protestant Irish hated him so. His speeches could be violent and abusive, and he could stray far from a strict adherence to fact, like all his countrymen. But then often he was only giving what he got in the House of Commons.

Early on in my political career there he took a liking to me. That was all the stranger because I remember as a child the terror his very name struck in my heart. One day our manservant Lawson, who had served in the British lancers, asked me why I was so downcast. 'Because', said I, 'I hear O'Connell is going to have emancipation and kill us all'. 'Don't be afraid, Master William', said Lawson, 'if O'Connell tries on that game, my regiment will run him through with their lances'.

He would call me over to sit by him when the House was in session, delighting in infuriating the old English Tories by having their young ally cross party lines to join him. 'Sit by me', he'd say. 'Don't pay any attention to them'. He'd joke and laugh, and next want to convince me that the Irish problem was not just about the prejudice of Englishmen toward Irish Catholicism, but about their disdain for all Irishmen, Catholic and Protestant alike. His eyes alternating between a twinkle and a glare, he'd lambast the English electorate for regarding 'them Hirish' like pigs. Any concession the English voter might make to them, he'd protest, no matter how harmless and how just, is something taken away from that voter's own feeling of superiority over the Paddies.

Despite his unhappy history with the Gregory family, which I'll recount shortly, he told me he had heard we were fair landlords, enjoying an attachment between our tenants and ourselves. I responded that I could not escape such an attachment, thinking of them as I do the most lovable and loving people in the world. Then he had me.

'Well', said he, 'has it not often happened to you to see on a Sunday morning this lovable and loving people kneeling outside a miserable chapel, while the rain poured on them, there being no room within, and they themselves being too poor to make it a commonly decent house of God?'

'I have seen such sights', I replied.

'And when you have gone to your own parish church on a Sunday, have you found it crowded with worshippers, and the rain coming through the roof, and no means of making it decent? And do you think a population treated with such unfairness in a matter that goes home to their hearts is loved by those who rule it, and can be loving to them?'

That image of a leaky, mean refuge at the heart of a people's belief in who they are never left me. Nor has its collapsing of illusions, like the weight of the old Catholic chapel roof falling in on itself, about relations between the dispossessed and their intimate masters. Nobody wriggles out of that most natural of unnatural pairings unsullied and intact.

O'Connell had formed the Catholic Association to fight the reigning order and sustained it with a penny a month contribution to the cause, collected by the Catholic priests. Nor did these boyos hesitate to use their religious influence to keep the pennies pouring in from their poor flocks. I heard that one tenant said his landlord could hurt him in this world, but the priest could make him suffer for all eternity in the next. Some members of Parliament wanted to put the priests on the dole from the government to buy their loyalty to the Crown, and lessen their influence with their people, who then might see them as privileged state pensioners. A desperate strategy to be sure, and one that went nowhere.

It was in the by-election of 1828 that O'Connell engineered the beginning of the end of the world of the Irish Protestant Ascendancy that my grandfather had sworn himself to protect. The occasion, ironically, was the promotion of the liberal Protestant member of Parliament from Clare, Vesey Fitzgerald, long a supporter of Catholic emancipation, to the Prime Minister's cabinet. The law required that with the cabinet appointment he resign his seat in Parliament and run for re-election. O'Connell decided to stand against Fitzgerald, despite being excluded from Parliament by virtue of his Catholicism.

Well then, the Romish clergy in the constituency threw off all constraints in their frantic efforts to get O'Connell elected. Fitzgerald's tenants approaching the polling place were subjected to the likes of this self-pitying browbeating from one of the clerical election agents:

> You have heard the tones of the tempter and the charmer whose confederates have through all ages joined the descendants of the Dane, the Norman, and the Saxon, in burning your churches, in levelling your altars, in slaughtering your clergy, in stamping out your religion. Let every renegade to God and his country follow Vesey Fitzgerald, and every true Catholic Irishman follow me.

O'Connell won the seat on the back of this sort of shameless manipulation.

The government was at a loss to know what to do with O'Connell then. He had cornered and well cornered my grandfather's good friends, our reluctantly Anglo-Irish Prime Minister the Duke of Wellington, and the Home Secretary, Robert Peel. (Wellington liked to say of his birth in Dublin that 'because a man is born in a stable it does not make him a horse'.) To prevent O'Connell from taking his seat was no solution, for he almost certainly would have run again and been elected again. The risk of sustained unrest across Ireland in that scenario was too high, and the issue was divisive in Parliament. The House of Commons had voted for Catholic emancipation more than once, only to see it voted down in the House of Lords.

Peel's backbone snapped under the pressure. He introduced a bill for emancipation in 1829, and it passed – a testament to Peel's flexibility, or his shamelessness. When he had been Chief Secretary for Ireland in 1815, he hated O'Connell so much he challenged him to a duel. The only thing that stopped the two from blowing holes in each other was O'Connell's arrest on his way to the duel. Now here they were fourteen years later arm-in-arm, instead of taking up arms against each other.

The Roman Catholic Relief Act of 1829 not only restored civil and electoral rights to His Majesty's Catholic subjects. It also sought to limit their exercise of those rights, to be sure. The franchise for voting in Ireland was raised from forty shillings to ten pounds, thus shrinking the electorate from 100,000 to 16,000. But nods such as this to the Protestant Ascendancy did little to satisfy them. On the other hand, it fuelled the chronic rage among Catholics who went on to press for the total dissolution of Ireland's union with England and downgrading the privileged status of the Anglican Church.

My grandfather continued to resist all this from his post as Under Secretary for Ireland, a post rendered tenuous as successive governments in London felt him more and more an irritant to smoother Anglo-Irish relations. With O'Connell labelling him 'the very demon of Orangeism' and his removal 'indispensable' to quelling unrest in Ireland, the new Chief Secretary for Ireland agreed to accept the position in 1830 only if my grandfather were ousted from his. And so, he was. It was a bitter, graceless end to a career of dedicated, canny service to keeping Ireland loyal to the Crown. A lesson to me as well about the perils of attempting to straddle the Irish Sea, with one foot sinking into the Irish bogs and the other slipping on the greasy surface of political ambition in the capital of the British Empire.

For Augusta, that perilous, ultimately unbalanced straddling was the impetus for all her lovely work. For my grandfather and all the previous generations of Gregorys, they would become the progenitors-by-marriage of an Irish literary legacy they could never imagine and would not have wanted. Augusta would write about the Irish mythological warrior, Cuchulain, whose frenzy in battle caused a 'warp spasm', transforming his body into an unrecognisable war machine. Sometimes it seems to me we Gregorys have been warp-spasmed into Irishness – not by rage, but by the conniving charm of O'Connell and his ilk, their Celtic siren song that only the rarest Odysseus can sail by.

I said earlier I knew Augusta loved me. Like a fool, despite O'Connell's parable of the damaged chapel, I thought my Coole Park tenants at least liked me. Or I knew I wanted to believe they did. As O'Connell himself recognised, the Gregorys were good landlords. But by the 1880s, when I would return to Coole from visits to England and the Continent, or when I would hear from home during my regular travels to Egypt, it was clear that meddlers were undermining relationships on the estate. The anti-rent campaign was taking its mean toll. A 'Captain Rentstopper' even threatened my tenants if they paid their rent. Many chose not to, whether out of disloyalty to me or fear of such thuggery, or a mix of the two. Some sought advantage in the circumstances by trying to strong-arm me into reducing their already low rents and decimating Coole's woodlands to burn in their hearths. Imagine. I had my agent turn back that idea and be clear with the tenants that I was moving to evict those withholding rents.

These people seemed to have no notion of the revenue required to keep up a large estate, and where it had to come from. Their priest at the time, Father Shannon, urged me to halt the eviction process and reach a 'kindly' settlement with them. Kindly! When this same priest's parishioners were refusing to pay him his Easter dues, because he was too friendly for their rude tastes with me and the other landlords. I felt I had to unburden myself to him and send a message through him to the agitators. I wrote:

> I must now tell you with deep regret that I feel so deeply the way I have been treated that it is my intention no longer to reside at Coole. I had hoped to have lived and died there, but I will certainly not expose my wife and child to the risk of vengeance and outrage. I mean to dismantle the house and to remove everything of value to a safe place, and if they blow up the residence I shall be very much obliged to them – I only regret that I have laid out very foolishly so much money upon it of late years which I did from the happiness of living among tenants who had I thought the affection for me which I had for them.

That scared them, and they came around for a while. Many of my tenants restarted their payments, but through the mail, so they would not be seen delivering them. They were bashed nonetheless in the Catholic press and threatened once more with eternal damnation. That was enough to dry up the rent flow once again.

The slackers in the viceroy's office at Dublin Castle were no damn help with any of this. Sitting on their fat arses in Dublin, they could not imagine that a landlord's troubles in the far west of Ireland, the name calling, the extortion, the undermining of Coole Park's revenues, the threats, the need for police protection – in some instances the outright violence – would ever really loosen the empire's grip on the place. They, like I, would not live to see Patrick Pearse and his merry band of misfits act out the Irish Rising of 1916. Had they, they might have looked back and understood as Cromwell did looking forward: support the transplanted English owning the land in Ireland, cultivate and expand the reach of the Anglo-Irish Ascendancy on their estates, or have John Bull England lose Cathleen Ni Houlihan Ireland to the romance of her Cuchulain warriors forever more.

I knew it was all crumbling to dust when some workers in the fields at Coole no longer tipped their hats to me as I passed. All together we are under that dust now. The Cuchulains and the Cromwellites, my family the Gregorys, Augusta's family the Persses, the other kind of Pearses – Patrick's – as well. All blending together into the Irish sod of their classless Republic.

Augusta absorbed all this in a way I never could. She imbibed Ireland. She listened so well to my naïve exhortations at the time we were about to be married. I wrote her then that 'I always felt the strongest sense of duty towards my tenants, and I have had a great affection for them. They have never in a single instance caused me displeasure, and I know you can and will do everything in your power to make them love and value us'. What she chose to do was love and value their world, their world view, their language, with all that intelligent affection on vivid display in her literature and her fierce creation of the Abbey Theatre.

She gave the native Irish culture and its modern manifestations a voice, and a venue at the Abbey where that voice could murmur, sing, and shout. She did all that after I was gone. Just as well. I admire her for that, though, and love her for it. Now that I rest in the Gregory family vault at Kiltartan, I suppose I am part of an Irish world both older and younger than the one I inhabited. I am no stranger to either of those Augusta worlds, but my time between the two was my time.

Figure 3. Wilfrid Scawen Blunt. Courtesy of Colin Smythe.

Wilfrid Scawen Blunt 1840–1922

> Wilfrid Blunt was a notorious, charming, dilettantish, anti-imperialist womaniser and a minor poet and essayist. Lady Gregory had an affair with him when she was a young mother early in her marriage to Sir William Gregory. She felt terrible guilt about the affair for the rest of her life, yet kept Blunt as a friend for the rest of his. His mother converted to Roman Catholicism when he was eleven. He followed her reluctantly a year later, only to reject the strictures of the faith – especially the sexual ones – as a young man and then return to the fold on his death bed. He enjoyed many romantic romps after Augusta Gregory, to the dismay of his long-suffering wife, Anne, granddaughter of Lord Byron. He seems to have had a remarkable ability to keep many in his network of ex-lovers as friends after passions had cooled. His daughter grumbled that 'life with him was a series of earthquakes and thunderstorms with the one compensation that no one could complain of its monotony'.

Augusta has the right to complain about the men in her life (although she did little enough of it). Especially about this one, since I had the compulsion to love so many of the women in mine, serially, or sometimes simultaneously, faithlessly but sincerely. The sincerity meant that I could often keep them as friends after the ardour had transferred to the next one. I loved and lost and loved lost causes, former lovers, Arabian horse breeding, Egyptian and Irish nationalism, even Catholicism.

My first love, my dear mother, betrayed me into this last cause, which I would in turn betray and then return to on my death bed. When she followed her friend Archdeacon Manning in leaving the Anglican Church for Roman Catholicism, she first kept it a secret from my brother and me. Thank God my father had had a happy death years before from a chill following an over-ambitious cub-hunting expedition. He would have preferred devourment by a cub's sow to what he would have considered my mother's fervid conversion foolishness.

CHAPTER 3

When she told us it filled us with unspeakable shame. What would my classmates think now that she had gone over to the enemy? It was the first and worst instance of intimate betrayal in my life and set a pattern I would inflict on others.

I remember wishing, childishly, she would have just kept it all a secret. I loved secrets all my long life. A way of manipulating others based on what you know and they don't, and then revealing it to them so that you reframe their view of the relationships of people and things. I wrote my *Secret History of Egypt*, the works on India and Ireland that exposed the hidden brutality and futility of British policy in those countries, and my own secret memoirs. All considered betrayals by some of my countrymen and some of my intimates.

I banned access to my memoirs for fifty years, then dropped it to thirty years so they might still have some bite in them when read. I guess they did. When the bloody custodians had a look after thirty years in 1952, they gasped and left them sitting for another twenty years in their tin boxes at the Fitzwilliam Museum. Perhaps they were scandalised by my revelation there of my affair with Augusta, by then idealised as First Lady of the Irish Theatre. Let them be. I am a connoisseur of scandal.

I was eleven when my mother converted to Catholicism. I refused to follow her and was desperate to have her abandonment of the Reformation kept as quiet as possible. By the next year I had betrayed it myself and been received – reluctantly on my part – into the Church of Rome. I was just a boy trying to please the woman. Then of course later I proclaimed a pox on both their confining houses to live a wider, wilder life. Sir William Gregory, Augusta's poor cuckold of a husband, predicted that I would die with the sacred wafer in my mouth. Secrets produce multiple betrayals. Perhaps honesty does as well, just not in as exhilarating a fashion.

After all the liaisons with their furtiveness and nastiness and heat and exposures and drama, I had thought to keep my relationship with my last and truest love, Dorothy Carleton, a sort of publicly respectable secret. Her guardians, my cousin, Percy Wyndham, and his wife, Madeline, were happy enough to go along with the pleasant ruse of my 'adopting' her as my niece. She was young enough to be my daughter after all, an annoying fact my actual daughter, Judith, was keen to force on my attention at every turn.

But the 10,000-pound legacy I bestowed on Dorothy, and my relieving Percy through her adoption of the 200 pounds per year he spent to support her, seemed to smooth any friction the Wyndhams might have felt over countenancing the arrangement. I know it lightened their consciences at the time as well to think I was dying, and that the cohabitation with Dorothy would therefore take on the cast of a nurse/patient, needy author/helpful secretary relationship. Yet indeed it was in everything but name a marriage. Those knew who chose to know.

Certainly, cousin Percy's Madeline did. She had been one of my conquests in the day herself, a tall strong woman. When I dallied with Madeline was a time when nearly all the women I knew well expected me to make love to them. Later her own daughter, Mary Wyndham, would fall into my arms. I came to think of her as my 'Bedouin wife', in and out of my tent sporadically over many years.

But back – or forward – to my beloved Dorothy. The road to her was a winding one, around not only the Wyndhams but my wife, Anne. On Anne's behalf the Wyndhams arranged a visit for Dorothy with Lady Gregory at Coole Park. The idea was to see if Dorothy and Augusta's son, Robert, might hit it off, so that I would then turn my affections back to Anne. My dear friend Augusta, however, according to Dorothy, undermined the purpose of the party by praising me effusively for my bullfighting courage and playwriting and my support for the Egyptian nationalist cause we shared in our younger days. Even Augusta's houseboy Yeats, in the midst of proposing to mesmerise Dorothy and read her horoscope, complimented the poetical nature of my contribution to the Abbey Theatre.

Neither he nor Robert caught fire with Dorothy. It seemed my road to her was considerably straightened by Coole Park miscues. I've wondered often if indeed they were miscues, or if the mistress of Coole Park was playing the covert matchmaker to influence who might succeed her in my bed. Later in my life, in my decline, Augusta and Dorothy became fast friends. Apparently, I not only could keep lovers as friends, but turn them into friends with each other, and not because of mutual hatred for me. A remarkable accomplishment for any man. Something of value from me that they recognised together must have lingered between them, and outweighed whatever hurt, disgust, and anger I caused them. I wonder what it was finally, and I fear I shall never know.

My passion for Dorothy feels now like the older man's version of my youthful passion for Skittles. Ah, Skittles. The scandalously witty actress Mrs Patrick Campbell told Yeats, as Augusta related to me, that the difference between men is not manners, or good breeding even. It is rather that some seem to have loved princesses and some sluts. (She is also purported to have said, of a homosexual relationship: 'My dear, I don't care what they do, so long as they don't do it in the street and frighten the horses'.) But Skittles, there was a princess of high order and a slut of the lowest pleasures.

It was said she got her nickname from her proficiency in a Chelsea skittles alley. She must have bowled over the pins the way she bowled over men, knocking them expertly into each other until every last one was prostrate. She was an elegant, rich, mysterious courtesan with many past lives and loves when I encountered her. I was mad for all her tricks and turns, blind to her using men of wealth and power to gain both. She was soulless to herself and sold to them.

CHAPTER 3

For two years and more after meeting Skittles I was convinced that the trifles of dress and vanity that occupied her were the things of most importance in the world, and that its serious pursuits were a mere waste of time. Daughter of an Irishwoman and her Liverpool sea captain husband, she bedded a fleet of grand English lords. Her mother died when she was four, and she eventually ran away from a convent where her father had placed her. But not until she had assaulted the mother superior.

Athletic and magnetic, she pulled life onto her slick surface with nothing beneath. She had me splayed full-body on that diaphanous, hard, unforgiving surface. When she cast me off like a lovesick schoolboy, I thought the world had stopped. But the Skittles passion went on with me. The other women – I loved them all in my way, but perhaps they were too forgiving to leave a permanent mark like Skittles did.

My wife Lady Annabella King-Noel, Anne, Lord Byron's granddaughter, certainly had a lighter, sadder touch. She thought herself plainer than she was and had none of the ways of a pretty woman, though in truth she had that sort of prettiness a bird has, a redbreast or a nightingale, agreeable to the eye if not aggressively attractive. Her presentation, indeed, I used to think was like a robin's, with its bright black eyes, its russet plumage and its tinge of crimson red. She had beautiful white teeth and complexion rather brown than fair, of the short-skulled west of England type she represented well. In stature less than tall, well poised and active, with a trim light figure set on a pair of small, high-instepped feet.

Without Anne, I would not have been rich enough to live the life of Blunt. The wealth she brought to the marriage allowed me to wander down pathways of the mind and the globe that would have otherwise been inaccessible to me. Perhaps that was why she was so upset when she found out I had supported an illegitimate son and an illegitimate daughter. My legitimate daughter, Judith, too, felt the money should have stayed with her and her mother. It is true that the little sins of the flesh do not themselves degrade where there is love, any more out of marriage than in it. Nevertheless, one has to – one way or another – pay for one's mistakes in love, one's surfeit of love, one's longer-term love commitments.

And those involved in love with you all pay as well. It's rather like a bank, the lending institution of love. Everybody pays in and takes out. Some wind up as creditors, some debtors. But at this institution debt collection is notoriously inefficient. I have walked away from many of its loans with quite a light heart.

Anne and Judith had their rows, too, with each other, and I with each of them. I'd pick my corner, usually with Judith. Perhaps I'm not expressing this familial geometry correctly. It was rather like a love triangle – different from any of my others since in this one the three of us did love each other as family, at least intermittently.

The irony behind this curious triangle was how difficult it was for Anne to give birth to a healthy baby, and then after all that for me to practice the paterfamilias role. It was in no small part the quarrels with Anne over how to raise Judith that drove me out of our home and into the political arena – the impetus for separation in the presence of the very being she had struggled so desperately to produce to ensure our union. The multiple, seemingly constant miscarriages while Anne was after travelling – in rougher circumstances than she should have – had already made us both miserable. I wanted, needed, a legitimate son and heir to carry forward the family name, and now fortune. The very pleasant truth was that my marriage to Anne meant my income rose from 700 pounds a year to 3,000. I could now indulge myself in luxuries unimaginable to me before Anne. And so I did.

But despite the enormous dowry she brought to the marriage, she could not give me the gift I most desired: a healthy boy. When she finally gave birth to a male child, he lasted only few days. I baptised him myself, Wilfrid Scawen Blunt, Jr Suffering from jaundice at the time, I nonetheless bestirred myself to bury him with my little ring at the Catholic monastery at Crawley, after the vicar of Worth parish, the bastard, had refused him burial because of the lay baptism. The friars at Crawley chanted, but I was the only mourner present for this my only son. God rest his small soul.

When the two girls came next and they too quickly died, there was dismal satisfaction that they were not boys. We buried them alongside Wilfrid Scawen Blunt, Jr Judith arrived next, a female success in a long line of failures. Anne and I left for the Continent shortly after her birth, I suppose in a miasma of relief but also disappointment that Judith was not a boy.

We left Judith to be looked after by Minnie Pollen, another long-standing 'friend' of mine and our family. In fact, I lent Minnie and her family our second home, Newbuildings, to make it comfortable for her to do that. Our families were inseparable for fifteen years. I am quite sure none of them, including Anne, realised that Minnie and I were lovers – but I really don't know. While Anne and I were away in Algiers, trekking across the desert by mule, Anne had yet another miscarriage. I was almost losing count.

Then upon returning home, we found that Minnie also had miscarried. I suspected it was mine, and cruel as the fates can be, it was a boy. If only I could have arranged in my life the right woman at the right time with the right pedigree and the right reproductive gear to produce a male child! But maybe reproducing something unfaithful like me in happy circumstances was just too distasteful for the female goddesses to countenance.

Minnie decamped to London to recover, and in her absence her husband John and I became the best of friends. They had a daughter who was my wife's namesake, Anne, but known as Pansy. Minnie recommended her to my attentions, because the teenager was shy and her mother thought I might coax her out of her shell. Minnie told me that Pansy was in love with me already. Alas, this little dalliance rather backfired, and Pansy wound up joining a convent where Minnie's sister was a nun. This was the one instance of my showing a talent for encouraging female vocations.

Finally, all this and more feckless womanising wore Anne down. Watching her mother deal with it embittered Judith, so much so that she wrote of me thirty years after Anne's death:

> Her devotion to this brilliant but wayward being is a record of self-sacrifice and self-effacement. Hitler and Mussolini were amateurs compared to him! His tyranny and spirit of discord eventually alienated him from his family, from most of his friends and from several countries [...] his temper was not improved by hashish and morphia. [...] utterly ruthless in love or war, loving no one beyond the 'mad minute', hating most people and ready to fight with a feather, life with him was a series of earthquakes and thunderstorms with the one compensation that no one could complain of its monotony.

My daughter wrote well, don't you think? The Hitler and Mussolini analogies are overdone, of course. But the heat thrown off by her roiling yet controlled rage is palpable, admirable. I had, after all, at one point threatened to elope to Paris with her closest friend. I take reference to my earthquakes and thunderstorms as a compliment.

Judith could not understand that for me, love was a kind of war, a kind of work amidst chaos, with amorous empires to be ever extended and then overthrown. My loves of women and politics and causes were in this way entangled. In politics I railed against the injustice of British imperialism, whether in Ireland, Egypt or India. None of my women quite appreciated how some men need to project themselves onto the world stage in such fashion – except for Augusta Gregory.

My involvement with the Lady Gregory began in earnest right before Anne told me that she was broken by my constant womanising. When I first met Augusta, she was a quiet little woman in her mid-to-late twenties, more plain than pretty. But somehow attractive still, with good sense and a fair share of Irish wit. Intense, self-contained, well-kept, mistress of her own internal empire, she put me in mind of an Irish Queen Victoria, if that is not a concept too disruptive to entertain. The Irish found the real Queen entertaining on her last visit to their homeland in 1900, concocting such ditties as:

> Ah, the Queen she came to call on us,
> She came to visit all of us,
> We're glad she didn't fall on us –
> She weighed more than me cow.

But I digress.

Augusta's much older husband, Sir William Gregory, kept her rather in the background. I believe it was December 1881 when the three of us first sat down together for lunch at the Hotel du Nil in Cairo. They had been visiting the pyramids and touring the desert and having Augusta fall in love with all things exotically Egyptian. As Sir William blustered on about Egyptian politics, I watched his bright-eyed, silent wife. She had been married for about two years, and their poor son, Robert, later to perish flying over Italy in the Great War, guarding an empire he did not love, as Yeats put it, was a newborn. I had been married to Anne for eleven years by then. But a spark was struck that day that Sir William never sensed.

Later, when my anti-imperialist passions had turned from Egypt to Ireland, the old man would instruct Augusta not to have me visit them at their St George's Place home in London *unless he was not there!* This was because he was so annoyed by my support for the Irish Land League, which was making trouble for Irish Protestant landlords like him loyal to the English Crown. By then Augusta and I had decided to end our romance and replace it with a saner relationship based upon our mutual interests in art and politics. Sir William, however, showed no sign of knowing about our romantic entanglement when it was going on or after it stopped, and therefore no fear that my Irish politics might rekindle it at St George's Place.

It was Sir William himself who first pushed me to get politically active. He praised my writings on Islam and urged my interest in the young Egyptian nationalist Arabi Bey. At the same time, he had been tutoring the young Augusta on Egyptian history and current affairs. So you might say he unwittingly created an Egyptian oasis where Augusta and I would rendezvous. Just as my obsession with Bey and the cause of Egyptian nationalism was heating up, his was cooling down. Augusta's interest in what some would consider a romantic lost cause followed my arc, not her husband's. We fell into each other's arms surprisingly I think to both of us, as a result of our mutually intense political idealism about Egypt and the Arab world. We found ourselves in a lovers' thrall for each other and the vast empty spaces and exacting, intricate cultures of Arabia.

CHAPTER 3

Love and work. A woman was always more alluring to me if she was, or could become, part of the impression I wanted to make upon the world. Augusta was capable of this, whereas my wife Anne struggled always to keep up. One day they visited Arabi Bey's house together, with Augusta carrying our banner, and Anne serving as her interpreter. Sir William told me that Augusta had confided to him that she was far more interested in Arabi than she was in Egyptian nationalism. Men and causes Augusta would elide her whole life – here mixing her passion for the dashing Egyptian revolutionary with her anti-imperialism, with her love for me, with my wife's utility to man and cause as her translator.

It is perhaps to Augusta's credit that Anne seemed to consider her the least troubling of my mistresses. It was as I was withdrawing from Egyptian politics in 1883 that Augusta and I decided to end our affair and began our long friendship. Maybe to Anne this affair seemed more like an international occupational hazard than others. I was so inflamed over the righteousness of Egypt's struggle for independence that I rejoiced at the news that Arabi's insurgents had massacred and burned the British garrison at Alexandria. I think I shocked Augusta with that. She was a restraining influence, yet always remained my understated, trustworthy ally, the confidante of my political joys and sorrows. On the Irish question, she was my tutor as much as my student.

Augusta was in a difficult position from the beginning about Ireland. She was born at the tail end of a large Anglo-Irish Protestant family in their imposing Roxborough estate in County Galway. Neither fully English nor fully Irish, these wealthy landlord families, whether absentee or persistently present, were the florid tokens of English colonial oppression to the native Irish, while troublesome, untrustworthy colonial cousins to many of their class in England. They lived privileged lives worthy of the Ottoman pashas in Egypt, an uncomfortable irony that sometimes seemed lost on Augusta, but was never so on me.

When she married Sir William, she became mistress of his large family estate at Coole Park. When he died, she succeeded him as landlord. She was good at it. Caring passionately for the land, she tried to be as benevolent as the land tenure system allowed to her Irish Catholic Coole tenants. She paid close attention not only to the land, but to the language, stories, myths and superstitions of those who worked it, turning all that into a new modern literature rich with the mysteries of the old world. Remarkably, she did this while conjuring with Ireland's struggle to become a modern nation of its own.

From early in life Augusta had been a kind of secret Irish rebel among her family members. She admired her great-grandfather, Colonel William Persse, who pushed for Catholic emancipation and corresponded with George Washington about planting the gardens at Mount Vernon. Despite her worry over what might happen to Coole Park if the Irish Home Rulers and Land Leaguers were to get their way, she supported me when I was sentenced to prison in Galway Gaol and later Kilmainham for holding an illegal meeting on their behalf. She would later get herself admitted to Galway Gaol and send me sketches of my cell she had made during that visit, which must have greatly disturbed the guards. She even sent me poems she wrote while I was jailed. 'A Lament' is representative of her passion:

> My heart is in a prison cell
> My own true love beside
> Where more of truth and beauty dwell
> Than in the whole world wide.

She loved me all the more when I said it was an honour to be the first Englishman put in prison for Ireland's sake.

I think Augusta enjoyed the danger of her Irish nationalism and the danger of her affair with me. When I first met her, she was only twenty-eight, married to the much older Sir William only as I said two years, with Robert a one-year-old she had left behind in England. But even then she was a small volcano hiding its secret fires. Many years later she would admirably edit her dead husband's memoirs. I always believed this pious act was repayment and contrition to him for her infidelity with me.

She related to men through her writing self, with so much ghostwriting and editing, so much shaping and managing of their stories, as she did with Yeats and the other preening lions of the Irish Literary Renaissance. She wrote her way into their lives, wrote her own stories and plays *around* them, in both senses of the word, and with all that helped her country recognise itself. The pen was her love wand and secret weapon. Augusta is the only woman I have ever known of real intellectual power equal to men, and that without having anything unnaturally masculine about her. She was a fascinating writer, something of a poet, a good speaker and lecturer and an entirely practical businesswoman. I feel the right to claim something of her success because I had so to say the making of her education. It's a necessary claim for the male ego in recognising a female who has surpassed it.

But we were great friends despite my ego and treacherousness and the affair. Our relationship lasted forty years, while we were lovers for but one. As I was getting older and my health failing, she suggested to Yeats a 'poets party' in my honour. Yeats, Pound and the rest all came to my home to celebrate me. Pound did the welcome. We ate roasted peacock, and they recited poems they had written for me. Few things in my life pleased me so much. It was Augusta made it happen, and then decided she'd leave the boyos to themselves and did not attend. She drew the group of male writers to herself, organised them for the party, set them in motion, and then made sure quietly, unobtrusively from the wings that everything came off splendidly. I could feel her presence and see her absence. This was Augusta's magic.

She was such a good witch, worrying over whether she was casting a right or wrong spell. She never regretted her affair with me, but it haunted her throughout her life. She worried that the most intense love of her life, her son Robert, would discover it and spurn her for it. That is why his early death in the Great War was actually something of a horrible relief. She wrote in a draft of her memoirs: 'with all the anguish of Robert's death I have lost my one great fear, of losing his affection – Now there is nothing that could hurt me so much to dread'.

The worst thing that could have happened to her also comforted her that she could keep her secret from the one whose knowing it would destroy her. Beyond her relationship with her son, she wrestled with this fear of what at least part of her saw as animal behaviour coming to public light. She expressed it most directly in her play, *Spreading the News*:

> I kept seeing as in a picture people sitting by the roadside, and a girl passing to the market, gay and fearless. And then I saw her passing by the same place at evening, her head hanging, the heads of others turned from her, because of some sudden story that had risen out of a chance word, and had snatched away her good name.

But I loved her most of all for what she nevertheless has her character Grania say in her drama of the same name. Thinking of her lover, Diarmuid, and their flight from her betrothal to the old warrior chief, Finn, Grania proclaims: 'What are any words at all put against the love of a young woman and a young man?'

And when we were no longer young, she loved me still. She was a great help to me in my literary work along the way, as she had been to her husband, Sir William. That help continued beyond death. She ghost-wrote an appreciation of me in Miles's *Literary Nineteenth Century Who's Who*, pretending it was written by another male writer celebrity, Richard Le Gallienne. She also crafted a new preface for my own *My Diaries* when they were published in America in 1921 – her compelling voice calling the Americans to me.

Augusta worked with Dorothy, the executor of my estate, to see that my wishes were carried out. They became such fast friends that Dorothy could write:

> I have just had dear Lady Gregory here for two days which was a real godsend. She is such a wonderful woman in so many ways and her sympathy and kindness beyond words – I was able to talk over so many things with her, questions about publishing Mr Blunt's books in America etc. which is the greatest help just now.

Mr Blunt indeed.

A strange man I was, always a heedless spendthrift and prodigal in the ways of love. Both Augusta and Dorothy paid a price for that. I thought of them as I wrote in my Abbey Theatre play of Queen Emer reaching out to her rival, the young fairy Fand:

> We two like children lost in a beautiful strange land,
> The land of one man's heart, where we alone are kin.

The Lady Augusta used her powers in that land to make it, against all odds, a more humane place. Cleaned up the pigsty a bit, one of her Coole Park land tenants might say. I am forever grateful she was such a spendthrift and a prodigal with her own talents and affections on my behalf. And she has never dunned me.

Figure 4. John Quinn. Public Domain, National Portrait Gallery, Smithsonian Institution; painted by John Butler Yeats.

CHAPTER 4

John Quinn 1870–1924

John Quinn was a New York Irish-American lawyer and patron of the arts in America and Ireland. He knew all the major players in the Irish Literary Renaissance and provided legal services for a number of them. He and Augusta were briefly May/December lovers; she was eighteen years his senior. On the Abbey Theatre's 1911–2 American tour, the whole cast of Synge's *The Playboy of the Western World* was arrested in Philadelphia for violating a statute forbidding 'immoral or indecent plays'. Quinn hurried down from New York to defend them in court at Lady Gregory's request. His long-standing disdain for the self-appointed Irish Catholic morality police was only heightened during his cross-examination of one of the witnesses for the prosecution, who asserted: 'A theatre is no place for a sense of humour'. He admired the way Augusta maintained hers through it all, and the calm, defiance and strength with which she greeted this and every crisis.

She told me that she should like to avoid arrest, because of the publicity. 'One would feel like a suffragette', she said. Always wary, was Augusta, of making a womanly protagonist of herself. Especially when, as was the case in 1912 and I was representing Synge's *Playboy of the Western World* in American court against charges of indecency, there were male Irish playwrights to be defended and Irish actors to be kept out of jail.

This from a peerless woman who was herself writing new dramas and translating old tales to revive Irish tradition, managing the young Abbey Theatre, overseeing her large estate at Coole Park, looking after her family, and adroitly helping to fire the rise of cultural, and yes political, nationalism in Ireland. If she did not want to be regarded as a suffragette, she was nonetheless a female force unlike any Ireland had ever seen.

But for all that she needed this American lawyer's help when she brought the Abbey Players to the States on tour in 1911–2. In Philadelphia, City of Brotherly

CHAPTER 4

Love, the whole cast of *Playboy* was arrested for violating a statute forbidding 'immoral or indecent plays'. I had to rush down from New York to Philadelphia, arriving mid-trial.

The strength of the case against our dramatic Irish guests can be judged from two responses I got while examining one of the witnesses for the prosecution. When I asked him if anything immoral had happened on stage, he answered: 'Not while the curtain was up'. An even more humorous assertion from this self-styled drama critic was: 'A theatre is no place for a sense of humour'. All this hubbub because Synge did not portray all his characters as St Patrick and St Brigid on the boards, and used satire to demonstrate how dumb the dumb can be.

Augusta told me she would sooner go to her death than give in and cancel performances of *Playboy*, even if it meant risking a loud, rheumy-lunged theatre riot now and again. Once in a rare while, when she got really angry about it, her Anglo-Irish Protestant Ascendancy came to the fore. She once told Yeats it was the old battle between those who use a toothbrush and those who don't.

When I first met her, at the dedication of a new tomb she had erected for the Connaught poet Raftery whose poems she had helped collect, there was none of that. It was my first visit to Ireland, my first trip abroad, in 1902. Out of my early love of painting and Ireland both, I had had a brief correspondence with Jack B. Yeats, W. B.'s younger brother and a painter of some note, about an exhibition of paintings by their father, John B. Yeats. (The Yeatses were an initials-heavy family. Beyond the initials there was the pronunciation. At first, I wondered why if 'Yeats' was pronounced 'Yates', why wasn't 'Keats' pronounced 'Kates'? But I learned pointedly from the likes of Joyce and Pound that English is always out to fool us.) So Jack invited me over and off I went. How lucky I was to receive a gracious invitation from Lady Gregory to attend a party, a Gaelic Feis, in memory of Raftery.

Whether Raftery, a poor, blind, Irish-speaking, itinerant, eighteenth-century bard ever used a toothbrush is unknown. But Augusta wanted his contributions to the Irish bardic tradition remembered, so she gathered many Irish literary stalwarts around her to celebrate a new monument for his grave. W. B. Yeats and his sisters were there. Jack Yeats decorated the day's programme with sketches of the luminaries. Subscriptions were sought to underwrite the day's singing, dancing, storytelling and flute-playing, and to aid the revival of the Irish language. The programme was blunt about the latter purpose, saying it was 'to drive from our homes the tongue of Henry VIII, Elizabeth and Cromwell'. Ironic, given the herculean efforts of Augusta and W. B. – and for that matter myself – to have the force of Irish letters shape the course of English literature in the twentieth century.

What was it about that long moment in Irish history that produced, arguably, the greatest poet, Yeats, the greatest novelist, Joyce, and the greatest dramatist, Beckett, of the century? Irony upon irony, Joyce and Beckett lived outside Ireland for most of their lives. All three were removed from the majority Irish Catholic identity – Yeats and Beckett Anglo-Irish Protestants, and Joyce a heretic continental exile. Beckett, ever the Francophile who wrote in French as well as English, when he found himself in France during the Second World War, would declare that he preferred France at war to the neutral Ireland at peace. Now from the broad, timeless perspective of my ghostly perch, I wonder was it that they were outsiders to Ireland, and as Irishmen at the same time outsiders to the empire of Englishness, and therefore free to hear the language shared by the two islands with ears attuned to other rhythms?

In *A Portrait of the Artist as a Young Man*, Joyce's alter ego Stephen Dedalus muses on a conversation with his dean of students, an English Jesuit: 'The language in which we are speaking is his before it is mine. How different are the words "home", "Christ", "ale", "master", on his lips and on mine! I cannot speak or write these words without unrest of spirit. His language, so familiar and so foreign, will always be for me an acquired speech'. Their very standoffishness to English perhaps empowered them to manipulate it, to juggle it, to play tricks with and on it, to turn it inside out and watch it right itself – to create new forms with it to artfully embody the chaos of the twentieth century.

Augusta was her own kind of outsider. While Yeats, Joyce and Beckett came at the dominant literary canon as disrupters to undermine and recast it, Augusta came from inside that domination to raise up the Gaelic and strangely accented English voices of the dominated. As a wealthy, landowning, globe-trotting, Anglo-Irish Protestant who married into an established aristocratic family, she was perhaps in a sense even farther outside the native Irish Catholic Gaelic tradition that Raftery represented. But she stood closely astride the culture and religion of those who laboured at Coole Park and lived in their cottages on the estate or on small country plots in the Gort area around it. She was determined to show the world the glory of a folk literature that was the heritage of, as she put it, 'farmers and potato diggers and old men in workhouses and beggars at our own door'.

She wanted to learn the language of that heritage, Irish Gaelic, to enthral herself in it more fully, but found its grammar difficult and abandoned the attempt more than once. In the aftermath of her husband Sir William's death in 1892, she spent more time alone at Coole and used it to perfect her Gaelic. She even established a Gaelic class to teach it to the Irish who had lost the language of their forefathers. She toured the Gaelic-speaking Aran Islands to get closer to it in its living form. Her interest in the native language and culture was rooted in her

CHAPTER 4

concern for local people's lives and her love of literature. She worked to improve the agricultural practices of small farmers. She saw her grand estate at Coole Park as a centre of social and economic development for her poor neighbours, as well as an elegant literary salon for Irish intellectuals. Under her watchful eye, it could indeed be both.

The land itself at Coole Park absorbed her attention and gave her back an unyielding strength. She wrote me shortly after her son Robert's death: 'The machinery of my life has not changed. Last month I was planting for Robert, now I am planting for Richard'. Richard was Robert's little son. Then in a letter the next month: 'Somehow the master's eye seems necessary. Even here, when I go to the children in Galway [her grandchildren] for a few days, I find something gone wrong in woods or garden – the wrong trees cut, or the right ones planted in the wrong place'. Her master's eye never seemed to blink, her eyelids never drooping from fatigue. She watched over the people and processes and institutions of the Irish Literary Renaissance as she watched over the plantings and cullings and replantings at Coole Park. The glories of both would be her legacy, cultivated in the manner of mother and master.

Those of us at the Raftery Feis returned to Coole afterwards at Lady Gregory's invitation. It was then that I carved my initials into the famous beech tree to add them to those of Yeats, Synge and the other Irish writers she had hosted there. She used that tree with our letters engraved in its flesh to intertwine her writer friends with the green life of her home. I recall that day so vividly because more than a decade later Augusta would write of my presence that it seemed she had entertained an angel unawares. It was she more than anyone who made me feel at home in Ireland. With her help, I reclaimed the feel of the land my parents had left. Then, with her, I was soon fighting like hell over who could feel and say what in Ireland!

I already touched on the travails of Synge's *Playboy of the Western World* when it travelled west to America. But they began at home. I was shocked and disgusted when Yeats wrote me in early 1907 about how *Playboy* had been shouted down by what he labelled 'the brainless patriotic element' over the play's supposed glorification of a young man who killed his father, and the mention of women's undergarments. He revelled in his father mocking the crowd during a three-hour debate over the play at the Abbey Theatre by telling them they lived 'in a land of saints – of plaster saints'. A physician told Synge at the second performance of the play: 'I wish medical etiquette permitted me to go down and stand in front of that pit and point out, among the protesters in the name of Irish virtue, the patients I am treating for venereal disease'.

About nine Irishmen out of ten are good Irishmen and are generous, kindly men, but the tenth Irishman is such a devil incarnate that he spoils all the goodness of the other nine. That tenth Irishman was surely in control of the district council in Gort when it passed a resolution over the *Playboy* row that prohibited children at the Gort workhouse from picnicking at Coole Park due to Lady Gregory's support of Synge. Suffer the little children *not* to come unto Augusta, who had opened the grounds of her home to them to alleviate in a small way the dreariness of their workhouse existence. The action of plaster and plainly mean-spirited 'saints' indeed.

The American tour of *Playboy* was yet more intense for her than the drama's wrangles back home. The company had been invited to the States to perform in New York, Boston, Washington, Philadelphia and Chicago during the fall and winter of 1911-2. Yeats escorted them initially, but early in the tour returned to Ireland and was replaced by Lady Gregory. I had to get them out of legal difficulties in several cities. The Philadelphia brouhaha was not the only one. In New York twenty-five audience members were ejected and two arrested for assault before the play could go on. Much to my dismay, I became the travelling counsel and fixer for Augusta and the players. I was on the American road with her, and she stayed at my apartment in New York between stands in other cities.

Augusta greeted every crisis with a mixture of calm, defiance, and strength that endeared her to me. I know she felt the same about me. During the tour, she told me that in my support of Irish artists and writers and the Abbey I had been her 'best friend, best helper these half score years on this side of the sea'. She later called our relationship a 'rapture of friendship'. Indeed, it briefly turned to an intimate affection, although I was forty-one and Augusta fifty-nine when she first came to America. I suppose she flipped the usual December/May arrangement on me. I felt ennobled, though, by our intimacy, as if her willingness to embrace me so thoroughly made me a genuine partner in all the grand and good things about Ireland she sought to preserve and advance. Her love redefined the borders of my soul.

As the troupe and Augusta prepared to go back to Ireland, they gave me a special gift – a replica of the eighth-century Chalice of Ardagh. They had it engraved with lines from Augusta's play, *The Image*: 'He had a gift of sweetness on the tongue. Whatever cause he took in hand was as good as gained'. The chalice with its inscription seemed sacred to me even though I have little taste for religion. And the words off her tongue to me sweeter than any of mine. Back in Ireland she would write to mark 'two months today since I said goodbye to America and you', complaining that she felt lonely for the leaving. She sent me a precious seal ring along with a rosary for my sister, but haplessly both went down with the *Titanic*. The washing machine I sent her, however, made it all the way to Coole!

I can remember thinking, well perhaps I am as well off without the ring. I had so many other romantic entanglements, and hers with me would have been scandalous if widely known, hurting her stature as Ireland's First Lady of Letters. She wrote me more than one passionate letter, but was cool enough to tell me that mine to her were going into her fireplace. I loved her passion, but I also thought that 'Coole Park' was an appropriate pun on her mind's temperature, forever holding that passion in check. Despite – or perhaps because of – her combination of fire and ice, we remained dear friends right up until my death in 1924. Every year at Christmastime I sent her three grandchildren a box of fruit and sweets from America. I wondered if they wondered why their strange old American uncle kept supplying them with holiday treats. Little did they think that the way to a grandmother's heart is through her grandchildren's stomachs.

As far as I was concerned her first visit to America was a great success, tumult and riots and arrests and all. It was a world showcase not only for the Abbey actors, but for Augusta herself as well. The American tour gave her the opportunity to establish her bona fides as a public lecturer. She was invited to speak about Irish theatre and culture as the Abbey players moved across the country and particularly delighted in doing that at what she called 'girls' colleges'.

She told me a story about her talk at Vassar College when she was still feeling new as a public speaker and fretted that her voice might not carry. The Vassar president told her he would hold up his handkerchief from the audience if she needed to speak more loudly. At some point during her lecture, he slowly raised the handkerchief to his face. Uncertain, she asked him if she needed to project more forcefully. Embarrassed, he responded no, he just had to blow his nose. She reported that the girls shrieked with delight, and the president told her afterward that he had held out as long as he could.

She had a clever sense of humour about her which she did not regularly display, but which she enjoyed having others discover. She chortled when she told me about a tailor from Gort who wrote home after attending the Abbey: 'No one who knows Lady Gregory would ever think she had so much fun in her'. She clearly had fun that day at Vassar, where the students had put on some of her plays. She said they were 'nice, merry girls […] as nice as at Smith's', the college where she promised she would suggest her granddaughter attend.

Augusta was excited by a sense of freedom, possibility, expansiveness she found at American women's colleges. That's why she imagined her granddaughter as a Smith student. She passed along a remark Yeats had written to her from Bryn Mawr. He told her a faculty member there had said to him: 'We prepare the girls to live their lives, but in England they are making them all teachers'. Remarkably for a demure woman who had come of age deeply and comfortably embedded in the British class system, Augusta was delighted by the unsettled, raucous, raw bigness of America. She marvelled at the wide, wooded beauty of the Hudson Valley on her way up to Vassar from New York City. She met both President Teddy Roosevelt and President Robert Taft, and left no doubt she preferred Roosevelt's muscular, energetic presence.

Her American connections went all the way back to the founding of the country. Her great-grandfather Persse had been a friend of Washington. She told me that the Persse family home at Roxborough in Galway featured a case of stuffed birds said to have been a present from Washington. A field on the estate was called Mount Vernon, as was a lodging her grandfather had built on the Burren coast. Her reaction to visiting the real Mount Vernon was: 'The Americans keep their sacred places well'.

I've thought that Washington's particular brand of rebellion – throwing off the oppressive political and economic yoke of England without abandoning cultural ties – made the United States a model for Ireland in Lady Gregory's eyes. His doing that while lovingly maintaining a Coole Park-like estate at Mount Vernon enhanced his status for her as a landed aristocrat of revolution. She could even feel a bit perversely superior because Coole Park was built on indentured servitude rather than the outright brutality of slavery at Mount Vernon. With Ireland and America Augusta and I glided along parallel lines in opposite directions. I was an American man drawn to the sometimes smothering embrace of Cathleen Ni Houlihan, while she was an Irishwoman enamoured of Uncle Sam's tophat freedom from empire.

I often recall what W. B. Yeats wrote me about Lady Gregory's daughter-in-law, Margaret: 'I sometimes think that the combination of joyous youthfulness with the simplicity and conscious dignity that make up what we call the great lady is the most beautiful thing in the world'. He could have said that of Augusta herself, minus the youthfulness when he wrote it. I do regret that she and I did not find each other at the same age, rather than she being eighteen years older. I suppose we were star-crossed because age-sundered lovers. One of the many ways life can be cruel.

But I loved her hospitality, the richness of her mind, and the at once understanding and uncompromising resolve she showed her opponents. I grew disgusted with the *Playboy* wilful displays of ignorance, the repressiveness of the Catholic Church and the squabbling factionalism of the Irish in Ireland and in America. My father raised me in Tiffin, Ohio to treat all things Irish with respect and affection. But too many of his countrymen had the manners of cattle, and I got sick of them. Not Augusta. Despite her toothbrush remark, she never stopped preserving and enhancing and advancing their culture.

I provided lots of money and legal cover for that cause, but she was its Holy Ghost. She generated much of the spiritual and intellectual energy behind the men who brought Ireland's arts and moral presence onto the world stage in the twentieth century. I believe her first love was always the landscape of Ireland, both physical and cultural, embodied for her in Coole Park and the Abbey Theatre. Wherever I fall in her love chain behind that, I am a happy link.

Figure 5. William Butler Yeats. Public Domain, Chicago Daily News Collection, Chicago History Museum.

William Butler Yeats 1865–1939

As the first Irish writer to win the Nobel Prize for Literature, Yeats is perhaps one of those rare poets who needs no introduction. Despite his sizeable ego, he recognised that his achievement was in no small part due to Augusta Gregory's unwavering dedication to steadying him as a young man and cultivating over the long term the talent she saw in him before anyone else. In his journal, Yeats writes of their connection: 'She has been to me mother, friend, sister and brother. I cannot realise the world without her – she brought to my wavering thoughts steadfast nobility'. When Augusta died, Maud Gonne, Yeats's elusive beloved, went so far as to speculate that the older woman had been in love with 'Willie'. Their strengths were complimentary. She was more focused, practical, political and diplomatic, while he lent a more emotional and visionary drive to their work. They fed off each other's energies in a tangled web of personal, artistic and business relationships that helped form the core of a new Irish identity.

It was the morning of 11 October 1891. I was pacing the Kingstown pier south of Dublin with weather uncertain as a child's bottom, as Joyce's father liked to say, awaiting the six o'clock mailboat. On it was Maud Gonne, whose love for Irish nationalism over me tortured me through a long life. She was returning from Paris, wild with grief over the death of the infant son she had borne that radical French politician and journalist, Lucien Millevoye. At the time she told me she had adopted the child, a lie to keep the liaison from me. Such was her way.

The ironic Irish sea god Manaanan Mac Lir aligned the dishevelled wandering stars that day to have her accompanied on the boat by the body of Charles Stewart Parnell. His body was being brought back from Brighton for burial in Ireland at Glasnevin Cemetery. Maud had disavowed the great man, the leader of the Irish Parliamentary Party in the English Parliament, because she could not countenance his high-handed treatment of the Ladies' Land League and his repudiation of violence in the fight for Irish freedom. (She would undoubtedly have liked him better had she known the coincidence that the port of his last escape from England, Brighton, would be the site of an IRA attempt to assassinate Margaret Thatcher in 1984. The Prime Minister was in her suite at the Grand Hotel there, working late on her keynote for the Conservative Party Congress, when at 2:50 a.m. her bathroom exploded.)

The extravagant mourning dress worn by Maud as she alighted onto the pier was greeted with scepticism by onlookers, who assumed she had donned it for Parnell in a perhaps self-serving about-face. She nonetheless joined in the funeral procession. I was uneasy in the pressing crowd and did not.

On the very first day I met Maud, I offered to write my play, *The Countess Cathleen*, for her to perform in the lead role. I even read the entire unpublished manuscript to her on an outing along the cliff paths of Howth Head in the summer of 1891. I begged her to take the title role. But she rejected what she inevitably saw as a distraction from her anti-English politicking. Her focus then was the campaign against eviction in Donegal.

The peasants there whose champion she was began to refer to her as 'The Woman of the Sidhe', our Irish mythological race said to dwell inside the mound-like hills of the countryside. Her statuesque, fiery, unworldly presence impressed both poor cottiers and townspeople, Celtic Irish and Anglo-Irish, women and certainly more forcefully, men. George Bernard Shaw thought her 'outrageously beautiful'. Katharine Tynan says in her memoirs that when you met Maud walking in a Dublin Street you felt as if a goddess had come to earth.

So, you can imagine my thrill when she finally agreed in 1902 to personify Ireland in my later, more militantly patriotic play, *Cathleen Ni Houlihan*. 'She could scarcely be said to act the part, she lived it', exclaimed the *All-Ireland Review*. Maud was elusive Ireland to me, rejecting all my proposals of marriage, loving others more, loving causes more. She was the wild Ireland I could never quite capture for all my pursuit of it, and her. I think now that was because the pursuit involved my trying to make her over into the gentle, cultivated stateswoman of my imagination. A fool I was about all that. But I found a different way to fulfil the challenge of my imagination. That was through partnership with the gentle, cultivated stateswoman who finally overshadowed Maud in my life – Augusta Gregory.

They knew each other and reconnoitred my soul in a delicate dance to determine what space each would come to occupy. They competed for rights to shape the kind of Irishman I would become. When I told Augusta that Maud was planning to incite starving tenants in Kerry to murder their landlords and steal their food, she was horrified. Her response was instant, coming as it did out of a deeply ingrained moral sensibility and a code of conduct that followed from it.

It was a code that reflected her class sense about how the world worked best – a sense that was self-interested, superior, and arrogant one might say looking back – but also interested in holding off darkness and savagery and dissolution. She wrote of our conversation in her diary in rough notes style that was at once thoughtful and thoughtless:

> we who are above the people in means and education, ought were it a real famine, to be ready to share all we have with them, but that even supposing starvation was before them it wld [would] be for us to teach them to die with courage than to live by robbery.

'Roses before bread?' Maud might scoffingly ask. 'One good robbery – sanctioned by the Crown – of native Irish land by the implanted Anglo-Irish aristocracy – deserves another', Maud would assert, sanctioned by her very different moral calculus.

After Manaanan Mac Lir's uncomfortable reuniting of Maud and the dead Parnell, there must have been another cantankerous Irish deity at work to throw Maud and Augusta together at the Nassau Hotel in Dublin. On one occasion Maud arrived there to find Lady Gregory settled into the rooms she herself usually took. Augusta told me she decided to take the awkward opportunity to make a maternal inquiry about Maud's intentions in regard to me. Maud's response startled her when she said she was only doing for me what she would do for her son, that she felt for me as if I were her son. Dear God!

But Augusta believed I needed to be married, and encouraged my last proposal to Maud, which was again rejected. Augusta knew then of my desperate pursuit of Maud's daughter, Iseult, and how my attempts to win her hand met the same fate as those with her mother. I had known her since she was four years old, and the serpents' tongues in Dublin wagged that I was indeed her father.

If Augusta believed I had become unhinged, she never let on. Rather, she played the matchmaker after I told her of my plans, finally, to marry my dear wife, George Hyde-Lees. Mrs Tucker, George's mother, was not supportive. She wrote to Lady Gregory asking her to help scotch the engagement. I suppose given my courting history the woman's concerns were not unfounded. But Augusta stepped up and blessed the union, telling Mrs Tucker that my intentions toward her daughter were genuine and upright. She even wrote to George expressing her delight at the pending wedding and suggested to me that George and I marry as soon as possible and I bring her out to Coole Park.

When Augusta passed away, Maud went so far as to speculate that the older woman had been in love with 'Willie'. Perhaps after all there was a hidden well of jealously in Maud. So be it. But it was Augusta's deep, deep well of kindness that sustained me.

CHAPTER 5

She was to me mother, friend, sister and brother. Truth be told, at a more mundane level she served as my personal assistant, typing for me, arranging for my living quarters and meals at Coole Park, instilling the discipline in my writing day. And so much more. For forty years she was my strength and conscience. I had never really known my mother well, and my famous, charming father had talent for painting and fecklessness in equal measure. With Augusta, I enjoyed the intimacy of a stable parent who did not fear, even encouraged, being superseded by the child. If at some level I wanted to turn Maud into Augusta, I saw in my new life with George a younger version of the Lady of Coole. Within a few weeks of our wedding, I wrote to Augusta: 'My wife is a perfect wife, kind, wise and unselfish. I think you such another young girl once'.

I knew Augusta well by the time I wrote those words. She reminded me more than once, however, that when she first asked me what she could do to help advance our movement to resurrect and vivify the beauty and dignity of the Irish tradition, I told her 'nothing'. Later, I advised her that she was not supposed to *write*, but to supply *atmosphere*. Imagine! All my devotion to spiritualist ritual bestowed no prescience on me with regard to the essential role Lady Gregory would play in the Irish Revival. Indeed, she became the compass point around which all the energy of it whirled.

Under her watchful stewardship, Coole Park would become the ground of the compass point. Perhaps I first began to sense all this when, to help me recover from my miserable love affair with Maud, Augusta invited me to join her as she went from cottage to cottage collecting folklore. She listened so carefully to the rural Irish English her tenants spoke about it. She would be the first to use that language upon the stage.

She understood that nothing was read in Ireland except newspapers, prayer books and popular novels. But if Ireland would not read literature it might listen to it, for politics and the Church had created listeners. Echoing the Irish version of English on the Abbey Theatre stage was what attracted the attention of the nation to our efforts. She held that attention by writing and producing more and more of her popular comedies and mythological dramas in the 'Kiltartan' dialect – English drawing on the grammar, syntax and ethos of Irish Gaelic.

She wrote those plays to keep the Abbey alive, all the while being maligned by our base half-men of letters as a selfish director pushing her own works onto the stage. Neither I nor Synge nor O'Casey nor any of the rest would have had the Abbey platform had Augusta not convinced audiences with her plays that the theatre was theirs. She helped me write every play of mine where there was dialect, and sometimes where there was none. She went beneath all that is individual, modern and restless, by harkening back to a pagan Catholic culture in Ireland. She brought it forward through the medium of her own Anglo-Irish Protestant sensibility, which itself was resisting in its death throes the modern meanness and meaninglessness.

How could I, or anyone else, have foreseen this grand accomplishment, nothing less than the reworking of an Irish identity for the twentieth century from half-forgotten and fully fractured shards of history, opinion, tales and taste? Augusta had reached the age of fifty having busied herself with writing two or three articles like many clever, fashionable women wrote. She undertook the dutiful editing of her deceased husband's autobiography and letters. Nothing there to predict her shrewd crafting of our country's literary mirror.

But she had secret ambitions. She once wrote that she feared turning out to be 'one of those dull people who edit books'. She abandoned editing for a kind of co-creation. Becoming a distinct and charming author in her own right, she was more importantly the Great Ghostwriter of the Irish Literary Renaissance. Through a wide range of interventions – with our writers generally and with the Abbey Theatre in particular – she managed to coauthor the entire movement. Her spirit coursed through the veins of everything we did, a bloodline of energetic dignity.

Augusta needed all that energy and dignity to make the Abbey work. We fought so many fights together to uphold our vision of how an Irish theatre should excavate the heritage of the country and propel its future. Refusing to stage some plays, putting on others, both kinds of decisions causing actors and playwrights to resign from the company. Taking control of the management and finances of the enterprise to ensure its survival, making others resentful of their lost authority. Fending off censorship from the government and the Church. Then when our main patron, Miss Horniman, withdrew her support, scrambling to raise funds by giving lectures, churning out more popular comedies, persuading other wealthy friends to step up.

Launching London and American tours with the Abbey company brought in needed revenue and gained us notice outside Ireland. Augusta led the demanding and controversial American circuit, battling at nearly every turn Irish-American groups that were offended by anything but holy cards on the stage. We were determined that the Abbey not be a holy card distributor.

In all these confrontations we fed off each other's strengths, which were complimentary. She was the more focused, practical, political and diplomatic one, while I believe I brought a more emotional and visionary drive to the fray. Sometimes I know she got annoyed with my ethereal nature. She once wrote me: 'you are like a puppy after a chicken when you see a new idea cross the path, tho' it may but end in a mouth full of feathers after all'. But I was hardly the most difficult of the playwriting brotherhood for Lady Gregory to oversee. George Moore and Edward Martyn, for instance, were cousins and inseparable friends, bound one to the other by mutual contempt. Augusta told me when I worked with Moore on our play, *Diarmuid and Grania*, that she feared he would injure my art. Perhaps she was right.

When Moore and I tried to write together she would direct us, much like she might direct actors at the Abbey, coaxing the play into existence. She had set up a bench under a tree in the Coole garden where we could sit and argue. When we became too boisterous, she would interrupt with questions and suggestions to refocus us. Moore recalled a typically diplomatic yet pointed piece of advice from the Lady: 'Let the play be written by one or the other of you, and then let the other go over it. Surely that is the best way – and the only? Try to confine yourself to the construction of the play while you are together'. Despite her wise counsel, a short spell of Moore and me together inevitably led to things coming apart. The wicked man did say that I looked in my old cloak like an umbrella left behind at a picnic party. Of course I said of him that he was a man carved from a turnip, looking out from astonished eyes.

John Millington Synge presented a very different personality for Augusta to deal with, more complex and self-contained. As I wrote in 'The Death of Synge', neither I nor Lady Gregory ever had a compliment from him. One night at the conclusion of her comedy, *Hyacinth Halvey*, she went home the moment the curtain fell, not waiting for the congratulations of friends, to get his supper ready. All he said of her triumphant *Hyacinth* was, 'I expected to like it better'.

He almost never praised any other writer, living or dead. For him nothing existed but his thought. Yet he was too sympathetic and simple in the ordinary affairs of life to think of him as an egoist. I often envied him his self-absorption. In this Augusta and he were alike – neither ever lost the self-possession of their own intellects. She always seemed indifferent to praise or blame. Theirs was a discipline I could never fully master. Her feeling for him was such that she visited him every day in his final illness and said when he died that she should have gone first. Augusta was mother, mentor, peer and servant to him, as she was to me.

In her zeal for the Irish language, which she shared with Synge, she invited Douglas Hyde, founder of the Gaelic League and later the first President of Ireland, to Coole Park. She wanted to encourage him to produce Gaelic drama for the Abbey. She herself had founded a branch of the Gaelic League and would collaborate with Hyde on several plays as she did with me. Unlike me, who counted five or six lines of verse written over several difficult, halting hours a good day's output, Hyde wrote furiously, without break, all day long. Augusta monitored his overheated labour, and at the end of the day would arrange with the gamekeeper to have the boat and guns ready for him, with the ducks on the lake.

For the sake of the Abbey, she had to manage many male egos with the most discreet, personalised care, and at the same time broker their testy relationships with each other. I don't know how she did it. Perhaps only a woman could. Perhaps only that woman could.

Augusta demonstrated the depth of her strength in how she faced the death of her only child, Robert. A mere three months after I had so greatly brightened my life with my marriage to George, aided by Augusta as I described, hers was plunged into darkness by Robert's fatal Royal Flying Corps plane crash in Italy. The centre of her universe was ripped out. The little boy to whom she had taught Gaelic, the young man for whose future she had built the cultural and physical vibrancy of Coole Park, could no longer be the epicentre of all she wanted to leave the world when she herself departed. In her despair she bestirred herself to request that I memorialise him.

And more than just a request it was. To her letter telling me of his death, she added a postscript: 'If you feel like it sometime – write something down that we may keep – you understood him better than many'. If I felt like it? I knew I *had* to feel like it, and I did – but after this 'postscript', delivered with a casualness to muffle its scream, I really knew I *had* to. Moreover, a few days later she passed along to me a second request, this one she said from Robert's widow, Margaret: 'If you would send even a paragraph – just some thing of what I know you are feeling – to the *Observer* – or failing that the *Nation* – she would feel a comfort'. Then almost with an apology for her directness, she sent me 'typed notes [...] not to use but to waken your memory to different sides of him'. Ghostwriting for me about her most beloved ghost.

I did more than my share of praising Robert in verse – four poems worth – embellishing the good qualities I knew he had to ease my dear friend's loss. This despite my own lingering uneasiness about Robert as a worthy successor at Coole to a woman who had given her life to the cultivation of high beauty and meaning there. I passed on to her reluctant ears long before he died her nephew Hugh Lane's opinion that Robert would not work unless he needed money. I worried that he had not the will to sustain his mother's legacy in a world determined to crush nobility of thought and the aristocratic society on which it is built.

But his mother desperately wanted history to regard her son as noble in thought, heart, talent and lineage. Was the desperation I sensed a response to rumours circulating at Coole Park at the time of his birth about that lineage? Her husband Sir William Gregory was so much older than she. A young Catholic blacksmith at Coole, Seanin Farrell, abruptly departed for America at the time

Robert was born, never to be heard from again. Sir William was said not to show much interest in Robert, and some believed that was because Farrell was the boy's father.

It was not long after Robert was born that Augusta met Wilfrid Scawen Blunt while travelling in Egypt with her husband, and their strong mutual attraction led to an affair. Certainly, she kept her liaison with Blunt from Robert, and only Augusta might know for certain who Robert's father was. I suspected a strange sort of relief in her with Robert's passing, although it could by no means balance out her wretched grief. His death did mean, though, that questions about any youthful indiscretions of hers, about his paternity, could no longer ever trouble his adulthood. His reification in her family and in public memory through my poetry was accomplished.

Despite our nearly familial friendship, Lady Gregory could on rare occasion be harsh with me. Once when we fought over some aspect of Abbey business she upbraided me: 'I think your proposal the most astounding I have ever heard of [...] I must preserve my own reputation for justice even in the face of unpopularity'. In the endnotes to her 1902 translation of *Cuchulain of Muirthemne: The Story of the Men of the Red Branch of Ulster*, she acknowledges me as her 'friend and critic, W. B. Yeats, for his kindness and for his severity'.

Sean O'Casey noted her two great loves were books, 'nearest her mind', and trees, 'nearest her heart'. She was unfailingly toughminded and stouthearted in fulfilling these loves. When a naïve reporter asked her how she had become identified with the theatre movement, she snapped: 'I didn't become identified. Mr Yeats and I started it. We *were* the movement'. Yet somehow she never lost a maternal sense of service and selflessness. I was startled but finally not surprised when an old man on the Coole estate offered me this tribute: 'She has been like a serving-maid among us. She is plain and simple, like the Mother of God, and that was the greatest lady that ever lived'.

With all her drive and caring, I wonder what she thought about the conclusion of *The Tain Bo Cuailnge*, or in English, *The Cattle Raid of Cooley*, which she translated from Gaelic. Hers was one of the earliest versions of the story to appear in English, in 1902. At the end of it, when the warrior Queen Maeve and the exiled King Fergus have lost the day to the boy hero Cuchulain, Fergus dismissively insults Maeve. He throws this at her: 'This army is swept away today; it is wandering and going astray like a mare among her foals that goes astray in a strange place, not knowing what path to take. And it is following the lead of a woman'. More than sixty years later, in a cruder time, the Irish poet Thomas Kinsella would vulgarise the insult in his translation: 'We followed the rump of a misguiding woman'.

I trust she felt the irony in this message in an ancient Irish tale she was reviving for English readers. For without her, we had no herd. Without her, there was no Irish literary movement. She saw us clearly for the fractious, cantankerous collection of male egos we were, and did not blink or spook. In stage parlance, she never dropped a line; she always hit her mark. This unparalleled performance in the history of Irish theatre was not rendered by any Abbey actor, but by its most committed founder and director herself.

Figure 6. Maud Gonne. Courtesy of Colin Smythe.

CHAPTER 6

Maud Gonne 1866–1953

'Women are at once the boldest and most unmanageable revolutionaries'. This remark by Eamon de Valera, one of the iconic leaders of the 1916 Easter Rising and eventually President of the Irish Republic, seems, shall we say, less than fully complimentary. Maud Gonne would have embraced it. Hers was a long life of self-styled rebellion. Targets of her revolutionary zeal included early on her own Englishness and then the British Empire, later the Irish Free State she helped establish, and prisons of all kinds. Her ceaseless work on behalf of prisoners extended into the next generation; her son Sean MacBride was cofounder and chairman of Amnesty International. Her personal life was as turbulent as her public one. She conducted a twelve-year affair with a married man that produced two children. Her later marriage to John MacBride was unhappy, ending in separation and his execution as one of the 1916 Irish rebels. Maud inspired Yeats with her bravery and beauty, but her radical politics clashed with his artistic sensibility. She would not accept any of his four proposals of marriage. She and Lady Gregory shared a deep love for Ireland but disagreed over how best to express it. Each was uncomfortable with the other's relationship with Yeats. Through it all, she tried to adhere to her father's advice never to be afraid of anything, even death, and realise what willpower can achieve.

Two young G-men were assigned to follow me around back in the day in Dublin when their English bosses still controlled Dublin Castle. At nearly two metres tall I was never hard to spot. Keep the troublemaker out of trouble, or at least go back to the Castle with any troubling intelligence about Maud. I almost enjoyed their indelicate attentions. I surely enjoyed toying with them. I had a three-act shopping drama I put on with their inadvertent help.

Act I was to parade into a big shop like Switzers with several entrances while they waited watchfully for me outside. I'd then blithely slip out a different entrance. Act II flowed from Act I seamlessly as Shakespeare. My G-men friends started trailing me into the shops, following me as I made my rounds. So I pretended that they were hopelessly ardent if annoying admirers. Casting a cold eye on both, I said to one: 'Young man, as you will insist on following me and you are certainly not ornamental, you and your friend can perhaps make yourselves useful by carrying my parcels'. Then a shop-walker threw them out of the store for harassing a regular customer.

Act III was still better fun. One day I headed upstairs to the ladies' and babies' department. The G-men dutifully tailed along. When I proceeded to rifle through the corsets, they strained their necks to look elsewhere. When their eyes came across other foundation garments, those two necks reddened over their stiff white collars. All the shop girls were staring at them. Their intelligence training had not prepared them to uncover these sorts of secrets. Just then the head of the department, an imperious, stout lady dressed regally in black satin, bore down on them to inquire whatever their business could be in this part of the store. They withdrew before engagement. Thus having evaded and then dismissed British intelligence, my little three-act play was an unmitigated triumph. Sometimes the small rebellions against the large oppressors are the most gratifying.

I was a woman in rebellion all my life. Against my Englishness, against the cramped moral standards of my day, against the strictures of the material world, against the British Empire, against the chauvinism of Irish men, against the soulless treatment of the poor, against prisons, against the brutality of the first supposedly free Irish state I helped bring into existence.

Perhaps it started because I never wanted to be English. Never Anglo-Irish either. Just Irish, like my great-grandfather William Gonne from the west of Ireland. Why was that? Some deep tribal connection? My given name was Edith Maud Gonne, after my wealthy English mother, Edith Firth Cook. But soon they started calling me Maud. From French, Old German, and Hebrew roots, it means 'mighty in battle'. They must have sensed that spark in me early. What better to battle than the world's largest empire in my time, headquartered on that small but omnivorous island to Ireland's northeast? I would serve no British queen or king.

I called myself 'A Servant of the Queen' in the title of my autobiography. It was the beautiful, wily woman warrior, Queen Maeve of Irish mythology I meant, not Victoria and her dour lot. Willie Yeats and Augusta Gregory made me into Irish royalty on stage, when I took the role of Cathleen Ni Houlihan in their play of that name – she who is transformed from a dispossessed poor old woman into a young one with 'the walk of a queen'. They understood that acting Ireland – enacting it – was my life.

Being Irish does not involve hating the English people, only the English nation. There are many English I like very much if I can forget they are English. My withdrawal from Englishness began early. My father, Tommy – my sister Kathleen and

I always called him Tommy – moved my mother and me from Surrey to Dublin in 1868, when he was appointed Brigade Major of the Cavalry in Ireland. I was barely two years old. Kathleen was born there. He was posted to Kildare, but he settled us in the posh Dublin suburb of Donnybrook. A weirdly predictive first Irish home that, for a person who had many a donnybrook ahead.

By the time I turned four my mother was dead of tuberculosis, along with the baby she had just birthed, Margaretta Rose. Tommy was soon gone as well, moving around Ireland and across the British Empire to Austria, Russia, Africa and India, as military man and diplomat. He always wrote us wonderful letters, and we wanted to be with him. We were orphans, really, finding family where we could. Perhaps that's why we fell in love so easily with the impoverished Irish families in the little fishing village of Howth northeast of Dublin where Tommy found a cramped house for our nanny and us in 1872.

It was a wild place then, no fancy suburb as it is now. We loved the sea and the hills and the high cliffs, all the heather and gorse and the great variety of birds. We loved being wild there, out of school, running with the barefoot local children, in and out of their mud cabins. The cabin walls proudly displayed the pictures of Irish heroes like Wolfe Tone and Robert Emmet alongside devotional likenesses of the Sacred Heart of Jesus and the Blessed Virgin Mary. I think our friends' parents and grandparents were cautious of talking about the meaning of such icons because they saw Kathleen and me as two little English Protestant girls, daughters of a British officer. Little did they know that Tommy was coming to regret the mistreatment of Ireland by the British Crown. He told us later that he planned to retire from the army and run for Parliament as an Irish Home Ruler. Sadly, that was not to be. Our dear Tommy died young of typhoid in 1886 at age fifty-one.

Back to happier Howth memories. I recall one day Kathleen and I running out of a rainstorm into a playmate's cabin with shoes and socks soaked. Our friend's mother took them off the two of us and laid them out to dry by the turf fire. Mind you, her own children had no shoes or socks to get wet. The Howth people were gracious and generous and embracing. After our short stay there, when Tommy sent us back to live with our relatives in England, we longed for the Howth heather and the freedom it represented. That was the Irish experience for us, and we wanted more of it.

Later, as a young adult, I would see the dark side of Ireland while trying to prevent or at least ease the evictions of tenant farmers in Mayo and Donegal. Their small plots did not give off sufficient rent to satisfy the wealthy landowners. I saw many a cabin door and window knocked in by the landowners' bullying toadies, sometimes with a battering ram. Families with young children and old grandparents were pulled out onto the road, their meagre worldly goods removed and carelessly dumped out on the roadside. The invaders would then seal the place tight so that the family could not return.

Sometimes the thatched roofs were set ablaze with paraffin. I met a mother and young baby who had been burned in that fashion after they managed to sneak back into their house and the fiery roof collapsed on them. They had the scars to confirm their horrible story. It was off to the workhouse for the evicted, where they would be separated from their children. More than anything else, these cruel scenes made me into an Irish nationalist determined to evict the evictors using whatever force was necessary.

That determination became my life. There was no separation between my will to free Ireland and the rest of me. My writing, my speaking, my organising, my beauty, my wealth, my love life, my family, my religious preference, all of it I drew together to hone the Maud Gonne dagger aimed at the heart of the British Empire.

Take my conversion to Catholicism, for instance. I got to know a young French priest, l' Abbe Dissard, through my French lover, Lucien Millevoye. They were both French nationalists, both devotees of Napolean. Their anti-English attitudes drew me to them. One day Dissard said to me that it was unthinkable that I should belong to the Church of England. I would not recognise old Victoria politically, he pointed out, yet by virtue (or vice) of my religious affiliation I was recognising her as head of my religion.

He was right of course. I had started going to Mass. I believed in reincarnation and mysticism. That was reinforced for me by Wille Yeats and his own theosophical leanings. He and I even used hashish to try to summon the ancient Celtic gods into our presence. The first time I met Millevoye I told him I was sure we had somehow met before, although it was not in this life. The ritual of the Mass satisfied my mystical and spiritualist tendencies. At the same time the thrill of participating in a 'secret' ceremony that the Protestant English had tried to ban in Ireland was exciting.

I knew, that many of the Irish bishops had never supported their congregants fighting for a free Ireland. For them, political servitude under which they had negotiated keeping much of their religious power over the people was preferable to the risk of a freer environment in which they might lose some of their authority. Perhaps that was a shrewd if shameful calculation at the time. I have no doubt that they are spinning in their celibate graves now over the 2018 vote in Ireland to legalise abortion! Back in my day, I had friends worried that becoming a Catholic would mean I would be constrained in my work for Ireland's independence. I worried about that too, but I never let it stop me. Ironically in all this, I have often thought that England's effort to Protestantise Ireland helped keep the Irish a distinct people.

Another attraction to Catholicism for me was the French Carmelite sisters to whom Dissard, now elevated to Canon, had introduced me. They were a remarkable group of women, fending off with the Canon's help the raging Masonic persecution of the Church in France at the time. I gave the Reverend Mother one of my dresses so she could avoid wearing her habit when she was out amid hostile onlookers. I had an invitation to come and stay at their convent, which I often did. It was peaceful there and I got to talk with many of the nuns who I knew were praying for my conversion.

On 17 February 1903, I was received into the Catholic Church in the Carmelite convent chapel. The Church's promise of contact with a world beyond the material one, my love of the caring society of women those nuns had created and the French Catholic disdain for the heretic English all were part of what brought me to that day in the chapel. Besides, now I was a religious sister to those Donegal and Mayo farm families I had fought for. I was more Irish because now I was an Irish Catholic. And … my relationship with Lucien Millevoye over, I intended to marry an Irish Catholic, John MacBride, about whom much more later.

How strange that my introduction to Canon Dissard and the Carmelites was through Millevoye. Hardly a devout Catholic himself, his brand of French nationalistic Catholicism served as battle gear against the hated Protestant Germans and English. I met Millevoye in 1887, when I was twenty years old, in the beautiful spa commune of Royat in Auvergne, fast by the base of the mile-high Puy de Dome volcano. Kathleen and I went there from Paris to 'take the cure', to enjoy the clear mountain air and the thermal baths. These were thought to help guard against tuberculosis, which had killed our mother and to which we were susceptible. The heady air and warm baths, the grand hotels and restaurants, and the company of well-off, attractive, vigorous health-seekers hardly guarded against a much more pleasant disease – love.

Millevoye then was a swashbuckler. Tall, trim, well-dressed, with a highly waxed moustache and dark, carefully groomed hair. He was charming as well. When I spoke up to get his attention, as I mentioned, saying that I was sure we had met before, he replied that it was not at all possible, because he would never have forgotten had we met. Only six months before then Tommy had died. I suppose I was unconsciously searching for a substitute.

Millevoye was sixteen years older, married but separated, with a young son. He hated the English as France's ancient enemy, and particularly because they had defeated Napoleon. He soon was urging me to abandon my debutante distractions. I had been presented at Court in Dublin in 1885 on the occasion of the Prince of Wales's visit to Ireland and had been much sought after for the rest of the season. He also looked askance at my aspirations for the stage, wanting me to concentrate on freeing Ireland from England as he was working to free Alsace-Lorraine from its German captors.

He proclaimed that with my looks and stage-trained presence and voice, I could be Ireland's Joan of Arc. To say that I was a young woman flattered and enthralled would be to say far too little. We struck what we both called an 'alliance', a pact against the British Empire. So our romance from the first was cast in political terms. Love of this man was in no small part a product of my love for my country. These two loves could not be sorted out, one from the other.

Lucien and I were lovers for twelve years. Our love produced two dear children, most scandalously at the time out of wedlock. Our poor little son Georges died on 31 August 1891 of meningitis at only eighteen months. I took to chloroform then to block my desperate sadness. But I never let any power on earth override my own will for long. With Millevoye's assistance I was able to beat back my addiction. I decided to leave Paris and return to Dublin that October to carry on with my grief at home.

By sheer coincidence, the body of the leader of the Irish Parliamentary Party, Charles Stuart Parnell, was on the boat I took to return to Ireland then. He had died in Brighton, broken by the vicious reaction to his own extramarital affair with Kitty O'Shea. I had never believed that his parliamentary tactics would liberate Ireland. Nevertheless, I had some sympathy for him when his Irish and English colleagues turned on him. It was a sharp warning of what would happen to me if my status as an unwed mother was ever revealed. Yeats came down to the Dublin quay to meet me. I know he sensed that I somehow needed him. Yet he and all the others assumed I wore black mourning clothes as a sign of my distress over Parnell's death. My most intense moment of personal grief at the loss of my firstborn was hidden under Ireland's public grief for Parnell. Mother Ireland's loss had subsumed my own as a mother. Who I was was defined for the public by her. I masked myself in her sorrow.

I memorialised my sorrow by building a large white marble mausoleum in France to hold Georges's small body. Such was the strength of my belief in reincarnation that I convinced Millevoye to have sex with me in the mausoleum, hoping that our dear dead son's soul could live again in a new baby's body. Alas, my hopes were dashed. Yet my spirit rose again when Millevoye and I welcomed our daughter Iseult into the world in 1894, three years to the month after Georges's death. She would grow into an intelligent, captivating young girl and woman. I always referred to Iseult and Georges as my adopted children. I knew only too well that admitting that I had borne children out of wedlock would make it impossible for me to do my patriotic work for a then very prudish Ireland. My own mother herself nearly became an unwed mother. Tommy married her the day before I was born. Later he would have an affair that produced my half-sister, Eileen. So the Gonnes are well invested in near and actual illegitimacy!

I wondered if my adoption charade with Iseult and Georges ever disturbed Millevoye. He gave no evidence that it did. At the same time, he never paid much attention to Iseult as she grew up. We gradually drifted apart. He was appalled by my association with what he called those 'absurd' Irish revolutionaries. He wanted me to champion Irish Home Rule through parliamentary processes. Despite all my love for him, he never really understood who I was. He focused more and more on Germany, not England, as France's enemy, eventually even backing the 'Entente Cordiale' friendship pact between France and England. His new friend was still my sworn enemy, and thus our alliance was dissolved.

Willie Yeats did not know about my affair with Millevoye until I confessed all to him, haltingly and tearfully, in 1898. Perhaps he had suspected it, though he never let on. My relationship with Millevoye was over by then, but I had no interest in a physical liaison with Willie. I actually told him I felt 'a horror and terror of physical love'. I suppose it was difficult for him to believe that, given the children I had with Millevoye – even harder later with what was to come with John MacBride. But he was absorbed in his art, and I was absorbed in my action. They would not mix well in marriage, so I turned down all four of his proposals. He then later proposed, again unsuccessfully I am happy to say, to Iseult. That made me at once more admiring of and more frustrated by the deep and ravaged romantic reaches of the man. I wanted to turn his art into action; he wanted to turn my action into art. He had many allies and counsellors in that effort, Lady Augusta Gregory primary among them.

It seems that Willie was forever writing and talking about me with Augusta. When I was thrown out of a carriage by a stumbling horse, he wrote to tell her that he nonetheless found me 'cheerful and talkative'. When I shared with Willie the full history of my relations with other men, he wrote her in a very different tone: 'If you knew all … you would understand why this love has been so bitter a thing to me, and why things I have known lately have made it, in a certain sense, the bitterer, and the harder'. The opinions about me in their endless correspondence did not all come from Willie. The Lady had hers as well.

I once sold my jewels to help feed starving tenant farmers and wrote that the Catholic Church taught it was no sin to steal the landlord's sheep and cattle in time of famine. She tried to get Willie to stop my activities on behalf of the abused, propertyless farmers. She wrote to him with spectacularly perverse noblesse oblige that even supposing starvation was before them it would be for the gentry to teach them to die with courage rather than to live by robbery. Spoken like a true Anglo-Irish Protestant landlord, basking in ignorant privilege and shameless cruelty.

She and Willie had a different attitude toward me when I was acting on the stage instead of in solidarity with the dispossessed in the west of Ireland. I mentioned that I performed in their drama, *Cathleen Ni Houlihan*. For its very first performance in 1902 I made my entrance as Cathleen striding through the auditorium in full costume, startling the eager playgoers. One of the young actresses in the Abbey Theatre company, Maire Nic Shiubhlaigh, later wrote that I was the most beautiful woman in the country and had personified Cathleen as the living symbol of a rejuvenated Ireland. Yeats wrote approvingly to Lady Gregory that I had played the part 'magnificently and with weird power'. For them, the art was the achievement. For me, it was a means to the end of arousing my countrymen to fling off the cloak of English oppression, just as the aged Cathleen flings off her cloak at the play's end to reveal a radiant and regal young woman.

A year or two before I played Cathleen, I met the man who would become my husband, John MacBride, back in Paris. He was an Irish hero of the Boer War when I met him, a fierce republican. He had organised and led the Irish Transvaal Brigade to fight alongside the Boers against the English in South Africa. He could not return to Ireland then since he was considered a traitor by the English and would have been thrown into prison, or worse. But he was warmly welcomed by the Irish community in the United States. He and I toured America together in 1901, raising dollars and enthusiasm for the Irish cause. It was on that tour that he first proposed to me.

I was thirty-six when we married in 1903, not ready to 'settle down', which I never did, but to have more happiness in my personal life, to share it genuinely with a kindred republican spirit. I married him in no small part, I guess, because the marriage was a sort of doubling down yet again on my own political commitments. I also wanted to provide Iseult with some family stability, which she had never known. Nobody among my family and friends, least of all Willie, thought it was a good idea for me to yoke myself to a man who was a narrow-minded traditionalist in so many ways.

Willie said I was lowering myself. There were the rumours about John's drinking. I told my sister Kathleen that I understood marriage was a hideous risk, but I was willing to take the risk at that point in my life. I told Willie later that I had done it impulsively, angry that Millevoye had brought his new mistress to visit Iseult. There was some truth to that. What is it, though, that James Joyce has his character Molly Bloom muse about her husband-to-be – 'I thought well as well him as another'. So I would be the bride of MacBride. But the drink turned out to be a huge problem for John, and for me. When I came to believe I could not trust him around Iseult or my half-sister, Eileen, when he was in his cups, that was the last straw. Our son, Sean, was born in January 1904, and I moved for separation at the end of that painful year. Then in February 1905 I filed for divorce.

I like to think that John and I did literally embody our hopes and dreams for Ireland in our son, Sean. Nonetheless, we tore each other apart in the divorce proceedings. They were as ugly and brutal as one could imagine. I brought in witnesses to testify to his licentious drunkenness. I tried to dig up dirt on his family in Mayo, even as my half-sister, Eileen, was getting ready to marry John's brother, Joseph MacBride. These family entanglements made it all the more painful. John stirred up the Catholic nationalists to denounce me as an unrepentant fallen woman. Worse than that in my eyes, he actually had witnesses called that claimed I was English, not Irish. When Yeats accompanied me to a performance at the Abbey Theatre after I had filed for divorce, some nationalists hissed at me and shouted, 'Up John MacBride'. I stared them down and set off a round of counter-hissing, all of it to Willie's dismay.

The heart of the fight was over custody of Sean. I was granted that but could not get a divorce in France as an English citizen. John was granted visiting privileges. I had to subvert those because I was terrified that John would kidnap the boy and take him to Ireland, where divorce was not an option and women had no real legal rights. John the traditional Catholic would have nothing to do with divorce under any circumstances. I decided to stay in France with Sean and raise him speaking French, a language that always defeated his father. John's French was so bad that the Parisians often thought he was speaking Dutch! I so regretted my marriage to John MacBride. I told the New York *Evening World* unhesitatingly that if a woman has something really worthwhile to do, marriage is a deplorable step.

Willie and Lady Gregory were abuzz about it in their correspondence with each other. She had written a pleasant little note congratulating me on the marriage but later told Willie it was a 'very sad' situation. At his plaintive urging she travelled to London to confer with lawyers about my case. I think she had been happy about the marriage at first, believing it would end Willie's pursuit of me. Once she had had the impertinence to ask me if I intended to wed him. When I told her that neither he nor I was the marrying kind, she seemed relieved if even perhaps more puzzled then by his multiple proposals. I suspect she felt I somehow failed him as paramour and now was failing John MacBride as wife.

Then came 1916. I was in Paris when the Irish rebels commandeered the General Post Office and the other sites in Dublin on Easter Monday. Willie was sending me the newspapers every day. He wrote to Lady Gregory to say that he believed it better for me to continue nursing the war wounded in France than to try to get to the trials of my husband and the other Irish rebels. When I learned that John had been executed along with the rest of them, I told Iseult bluntly that he had been shot to death. They unfortunately had always been stepfather/stepdaughter adversaries. She had accused him of inappropriate behaviour with her, and that was that.

Then I went to Sean who was only twelve years old, and I remember he was building a little boat. I said that his father had died for our country, and that even though he did not always behave well toward us, he was now a hero. I don't think Sean knew what to make of it all at the time, losing a father he never really had. His anti-English classmates in Paris celebrated the insurrectionists' courage in the face of the firing squad, especially his father's disdainful refusal of a blindfold. He found himself with a new status with that important constituency in his world.

I felt that John had atoned for his shabby treatment of our family during his life by embracing a death for Ireland that I believe he had ever desired at some level. I kept all the articles, profiles, and poems written about John and his brave Easter Rising compatriots for Sean so that, as he grew, he would see the way his father's sacrifice had been received. I started referring to myself as 'Madam MacBride'. That was a way for me to honour John and keep my connection to him without sounding too wifely as 'Mrs MacBride'. I had a pride in John after his death that I could not feel when he was alive. My ghostly husband became a more suitable spouse than the incarnate one.

Lady Gregory and Willie did not know what to make of Easter Monday and John's execution. Her first reaction was to offer Willie her opinion that it must be a release for me. She also wrote to her former lover, Wilfrid Scawen Blunt, expressing her unease that compared to the rebels who had given their lives, literary nationalists such as herself and Willie and the rest of the Coole Park cadre would seem insincere, too given to compromise. A well-founded fear, that. She was initially appalled by the looting in Dublin, and worried about follow-up attacks on Coole Park.

But for her and Yeats, as for so many others, the rushed firing-squad executions of the Easter Rising's leaders reshaped their attitude toward the rebellion. Two of them, Patrick Pearse and Thomas MacDonagh, had been Abbey playwrights. A young Abbey actor who was a favourite of Augusta's, Sean Connolly, was among those killed in the fighting. She seemed to sense that now Ireland had its new martyrs, whose sacrifice would lead eventually to a final reckoning with its coerced place in the British Empire. She could not help but be unsettled at the thought of Irishmen fighting their countrymen who had joined the British armed forces. At the time her only child, Robert, was serving in the Royal Flying Corps, patrolling the English coast around Dover to fend off German planes.

Willie's 'Easter 1916' poem, with its lines about everything being 'changed, changed utterly: A terrible beauty is born', could have been written by her. The both of them came to understand that their long-held dream to unite Ireland by reviving its ancient Celtic heritage without direct grappling with its independent integrity as a nation had been surpassed. Forces had been set loose that neither the walls of the Abbey Theatre nor Willie's elegant couplets could contain. His frustration with it all spilled over in his petulant reference to John in the poem as 'a drunken, vainglorious lout'. He knew, or should have, that I would henceforth be caught up in promoting the heroic image of John. Willie had lost me again, and his vision of the Irish future, in one stroke. Lady Gregory declared the poem 'extraordinarily impressive', while I thought it was hardly worthy of Willie's talent or its exalted subject.

His service in the Irish Free State Senate was another episode unworthy of him. The treaty that established the Free State after our war of independence in 1919–21 was opposed by those who wanted a fully independent republic with no continuing connections to the British Empire, no oath of allegiance to the Crown. This tension eventually led to our tragic, vicious civil war in 1921–2. Sean and I wound up on the republican side. Yeats and Lady Gregory supported the Free State. He lent it his status by becoming a senator when it was executing scores of Irish republicans, allowing hunger strikers to starve to death, and holding thousands of prisoners for months after the Free-Staters had won the war.

I protested their vile treatment of their former comrades-in-arms and found myself thrown into prison several times in the bargain. I actually served twenty days in Kilmainham Jail at one point. They released me only after I too went on hunger strike. The Free State poohbahs did not want to be responsible for the death of 'Ireland's Joan of Arc'. The original Joan, as we know, fared less well at the hands of her ungrateful countrymen. Perhaps I should consider myself lucky.

I found I could always forgive Willie despite his political sins, weighed in the balance of his poetic genius. Selfishly, maybe that is because I felt I was one source of that genius. After all, what *caused* Willie to write, what did he write *about* and for *whom*? As the literary critics have recognised, I was often his inspiration, subject and audience. By contrast, Augusta Gregory was his mere enabler. Or perhaps I should give her more credit, at least on the theatre side of the house, so to speak. I often thought that she and I were both father figures to Willie's mothering of his different literary children.

CHAPTER 6

As I wrote to him in 1911:

Our children were your poems of which I was the Father sowing the unrest & storm which made them possible & you the mother who brought them forth in suffering & in the highest beauty and our children had wings –

You and Lady Gregory have a child also *the theatre company* & Lady Gregory is the Father who holds you to your duty of motherhood in the marriage style. That child requires much feeding & looking after. I am sometimes jealous for my children.

Augusta did like to go on about her side of the family. When Willie sent me a copy of her *Our Irish Theatre* book, I told him I thought it a bit long and tedious and egotistical. But I also had to admit to him my admiration for her courage and staying power.

Augusta and I shared those latter traits I'd say, especially as mothers who had both lost sons, albeit in very different circumstances – mine in infancy and hers in World War I. After that, courage and staying power are required to go on and do anything at all in this world, never mind building a recalcitrant country. She and I could bring people together, working around that recalcitrance. We were self-styled grand convenors. She had all her literary men down to Coole Park all the time, instilling a shared national purpose in that fanfare of wild trumpeter swans at Coole. Willie spent some twenty summers there. I understood that people work according to their own temperaments, and was happy to enlist artists, academics, clerics, socialists and militants – both men and women – to come together for Irish liberation.

Unlike Augusta, my deepest cooperation and friendships were with women; founding and growing the Daughters of Ireland are among my proudest accomplishments. I never very explicitly agitated for female equality, but I trust that my political activism and writings speak to my certainty that I and other women could do what it had foolishly been the province of men alone to do. You could say that Lady Gregory demonstrated that as well. The difference, however, is that I led other women in the demonstration, whereas she ignored them in her quest to serve as First Lady of the male pack.

Mind you, I always felt myself a lady. Nothing wrong with that. Even as an old woman I wore well-cut gowns made in Paris and embellished my hair with gold ornaments. Too many of the Irish revolutionary woman were just dowdy, bad for the cause. I did sometimes feel guilty for not patronising Irish industries in my choice of wardrobe. Yet I never thought beauty a sin. James Joyce, whom I knew in Paris – an arrogant enough fellow and a smutty writer much of the time – has me being auctioned off in his *Finnegans Wake*: 'Gowan, Gawin and

Gonne'. The cheek of the man. My revenge on him is that I'm sure he realised I'd fetch a high price.

What was it that professor who wrote a book about my Sean said of me? It was Caoimhe Nic Dhaibheid, I think. When she was asked about Irish historical figures she'd want to have over for lunch, she said I was one, because she wanted to find out what all the fuss was about. Well, I hope those of you who have read my musings here will have a sense of that. Willie Yeats surely knew what all the fuss was about, uncomfortable as it made him. Augusta Gregory knew too, but sometimes wanted to pretend she didn't.

On the very first page of my autobiography, *A Servant of the Queen*, I recalled returning to Dublin from Mayo after defending the people there in their land wars. A cheering crowd and a band saw me off at the train station. Looking out from the train window at the darkening bogland I suddenly saw a tall, beautiful woman with dark brown hair blown on the wind and I knew it was Cathleen Ni Houlihan. She was springing over the wet surface of the bogs across little white stones. I heard a voice say: 'You are one of the little white stones on which the feet of the Queen have rested on her way to freedom'. I like to think I made a right splash as my little stone was set down under her feet.

Figure 7. Hugh Lane. Courtesy of Colin Smythe.

CHAPTER 7

Hugh Lane 1875–1915

Hugh Lane was Lady Gregory's nephew, the son of her beautiful older sister, Adelaide. An art dealer and impresario whose collection would preoccupy Augusta for much of her adult life, he died young in the 7 May 1915 German U-boat attack on the *Lusitania*. Raised in England, he felt out of place when his mother would take him on holiday to her and Augusta's family home at Roxborough in Galway. His brothers and cousins would spend their time there hunting and sporting around the estate, while he found himself absorbed by the paintings, decorations, and fancy clothes about the house. He grew up to make and lose fortunes buying and selling paintings. All the while he stayed close to his aunt Augusta, who championed his idea to donate part of his valuable trove of them to the National Gallery of Ireland and the Dublin Municipal Gallery. After his death, Lady Gregory would fight ferociously and persistently with the British government over what she saw as its moral obligation to respect his stated final wish, even if not legally binding, to have the works shown in Dublin, not London. Her tireless campaign came to fruition more than a quarter century after her own death, when the two nations agreed to divide the collection in half and swap the paintings every five years for display in both capitals.

Cork it was where the story started, and right off its coast where it ended. So close. Ireland's misted form floating there, just beyond my grasp. A deadly metaphor for my relationship with the place, I suppose.

The German torpedo slammed into the *Lusitania* early in the afternoon of 7 May 1915. Twenty minutes later, the liner had gone down with 1,200 of its passengers and crew. I was one of them, at age thirty-nine. Drowning near Cork. The kind of crude pun that so delights the Irish. As the ship sank, I said to Lady Allen, who would survive but cruelly lose both her daughters to the cold Atlantic, that I was going to find some new American friends I had just made, adding that this was a sad end for us all.

CHAPTER 7

I was calm, though. When Yeats had read my horoscope several years earlier, he gently indicated that I might be wise not to expect a long life. He thoughtlessly mentioned that to my dear aunt, Lady Gregory, as well. Yeats' prediction and the poor health of most of my siblings as they aged convinced me that I had to hurry life and work, for a premature close was hurrying toward me. If, as some said, I burned too hot, pushed too hard, badgered too insistently, well, I had reason, had I not?

Although I always anticipated a short life, I never avoided the risks that might bring it about. I had been in New York assessing the value of some paintings for Lloyds of London. Such jobs were just a way for me to get money to support my own art collecting. Nonetheless I found I enjoyed New York. My Irish-American friend and art impresario rival, John Quinn, raised my spirits with collegial dinners and theatre visits and rides in the country. He was right in telling Lady Gregory that I was vastly relieved to be away from the war gloom of London – the wounded and the dread of it all – and instead at play amid the cultural attractions of New York City. I would have stayed on longer in the heady American hubbub, but I had committed to meetings back in London.

I felt I had to keep those commitments even after Quinn protested it was foolish to sail back across the Atlantic on a British-registered ship like the *Lusitania*, for it could attract German submarines. The morning I departed from New York harbour, 1 May 1915, the German embassy in Washington ran a notice in major American newspapers declaring that those sailing through the war zone on ships registered to Great Britain or it allies 'do so at their own risk'. Buoyant from my gay stay in New York, I dismissed this as Hunnish chest-thumping. I never imagined that it would be one of their torpedoes would plunge me to the early death I did anticipate, almost within sight of where I was born.

I am a kind of accidental yet rooted Cork Irishman both by death and birth. On my father's side, three of my ancestors had been Lord Mayor of Cork. Seven had been elected High Sheriff. My parents were temporarily staying in the village of Douglas, a few kilometres from Cork City, when I was born. My father's aunt had bequeathed him a property there. Although my own aunt Augusta would cringe to hear me say it, the property's name, Ballybrack, always sounded to me vaguely like some ancient Gaelic sport. My parents were sorting through the place while they awaited my arrival. Shortly thereafter they hastened back to our home in Bath. I never set a foot on solid ground in Cork again, although I likely set no foot there as a newborn in the first instance.

My mother, Adelaide Persse, was Lady Gregory's sister, twelve years older. She was the most beautiful of the Persse sisters. Unlike the plainer Augusta, she was thought likely to attract a mate of wealth and distinction. James Lane, my

Anglican clergyman father, was not that. When my grandparents' old nurse heard that Adelaide was betrothed to a Lane, she worried that names such as Field, Street and Lane were often given to foundlings. Six years younger than Adelaide, James had to be married to my mother at a chapel off the Persse's Roxborough estate because of her family's disapproval of the union.

That it ever happened at all is astounding. They were kept apart by both their families for three years before the marriage to test what was thought to be their questionable commitment to each other. Aunt Augusta speculated, when the marriage faltered and they separated, that they had not had an opportunity to really get to know each other before they wed because of the imposed 'distant engagement'. What they shared most ardently, she believed, was a desire to demonstrate their parents had been mistaken about the appropriateness and strength of their bond.

As they grew apart, my mother began travelling without my father, often with her children, including me, in tow. My aunt Augusta helped bankroll her older sister's odysseys. As a result of all the moving around, none of us had a chance at a proper, formal education. I was always uncomfortable with my own limited grasp of literature, history, mathematics. If some found my conversational delivery energetic, charming, engaging, little did they know I was maniacally filling holes that my poor schooling had dug for me.

When my mother would return with us to her childhood home at Roxborough for a visit, I always felt out of place. My brothers and cousins spent their time at the estate hunting and cavorting. Culture for them was about riding and shooting well. My grandmother Persse forbade my mother and her other children from reading novels until they were eighteen. Hardly an encouraging start for my aunt Augusta's literary career. It's no wonder that my family was out chasing foxes across western Ireland, while I was absorbed in the family paintings and decorations at Roxborough, and in dressing dolls and dressing up myself in fancy clothes I found about the place. Even then for me culture was about seeing beautiful things, having them at hand, wearing them or attaching them to myself, and later possessing them. These proclivities certainly set me apart – from my family but also from Ireland, where family involvement was most intense during our visits.

My mother recognised, even sympathised with, my shunning of reading and writing and my interest in visual art and artifice. In Ireland, where glib talk and flowing prose are the standard measures of intellectual worth, this was yet another mark of a queer, un-Irish consciousness. But back in England my mother encouraged these appetites, engaging an elderly picture restorer to tutor me in her craft. Mrs Hopkins would never accept payment for her trouble, but only the occasional bottle of port and package of biscuits in recompense. We learned later she had starved to death. A deadly metaphor of a different kind, this one early in life, for my all-consuming relationship with the art world.

While Lady Gregory had supported my mother's wanderings, she also kindly introduced me into the world of art dealing. If my mother's unwillingness to stay home, subsidised by Augusta, was the main cause of my being unschooled, perhaps my aunt felt obligated to help me find a profession that did not require a gentleman's education – although art dealing could hardly be dignified as a 'profession'. At any rate, it was Augusta who got me my first job at Martin Colnaghi's London art gallery, salary a pound a week.

I made and lost fortunes over my lifetime of buying and selling paintings. I got into the business at just the right time. Land prices and productivity were falling across England and Ireland, estate revenues plummeting, due to the import of cheap American grain. In Ireland especially, the land wars and the withholding of rents by tenants radically reduced incomes. Selling paintings, often on the low side, became one way to keep old family landholdings intact. Thus was my orientation to the art market. It set the frame, if you will, for how I would operate and how I would be seen. That frame accommodated two quite different portraits.

My love for the art I bartered was genuine. My friend Henry Tonks, surgeon and painter, described me with surgical precision as having 'an almost morbid desire to surround himself with the most beautiful objects possible'. Why he found that desire morbid I do not understand – probably the surgeon's burden. To me it was the most enlivening thing, the core of my life. Truth be told, the paintings always mattered more than people. This could lead, not surprisingly, to strained relations, to a sense that there was something if not morbid, 'off', about me. Yet I would say I was truly selfless in my concern to gather up and show forth the beautiful.

The painter Dermod O'Brian was one of the few who understood. He said that I was 'one of those personalities so abnormal in his passion for the beautiful, in whom unlimited generosity amounted almost to a mania, that all his life he was apt to be misunderstood and his motives queried by that huge majority of us who think first of self'. My friends would tell you I even gave away art objects to visitors to my home in London, Lindsey House, if they expressed interest in them. The famous actress Ellen Terry was one beneficiary of my generosity. She left with a Chinese crystal figure she thought particularly dramatic.

Collect and disburse. These seem to be the two verbs that best characterise my life. Sometimes I did both in such a frenzy that I was not sure what I had. Was a piece an original, a fraud, or somewhere in between? I was usually an acute judge of the provenance of a painting, but never an unsure one. Sir Frederic

Burton told my aunt Augusta: 'I have never in all my life been able to have the same courage in my opinion as that young man'. That stubborn, if occasionally ill-informed, courage, combined with my impulse to have a beautiful painting reside with me, could convince me I had found an original when I had not. So be it. A bit of gentle fraud in the larger interest of true art is not such a bad thing.

I myself knowingly engaged in it to good purpose to assist aristocratic patrons who found themselves pressed for revenue. For those who understandably were embarrassed to have the world know of their need for money, I would buy their painting and supply a copyist who would make a perfect replica that nobody but a few experts on close examination could tell was not the original. The wider world got access to a masterpiece, and an aristocratic family got to preserve its dignity and keep a settled wall in its drawing room intact. Many more enthusiasts might enjoy the original, and those few who saw the copy when they visited their friend's grand house would enjoy it as well. If all art is in some way a fraudulent version of the real world, why not perpetrate a touch of fraud upon art to make its enjoyment more available?

And not more available to the moneyed few only. Too many Dubliners were surprised that it was I who pushed the Municipal Gallery to keep its doors open in the evening and on weekends so working men and women would thereby have an opportunity to develop their aesthetic sensibilities, and a greater appreciation for the cultural endowment of their country. When the Dublin Corporation and its Libraries Committee could not agree over budget for the new gallery, I and other supporters filled in the gap so that the doors would not be closed to any Irish citizen while the dispute was worked out.

I will admit I could be appalled by what our standard Irish Catholic could get up to with his dogma – religious and political – and his drink. I learned from Augusta Gregory that if Ireland were to stop fumbling in its own greasy till, as Yeats put it, and reconstruct its grander identity, it was those who had the means and a broad generosity of spirit who would have to build the workshop and do much of the work.

My aunt Augusta took on that work with an unyielding commitment of her generous spirit. It took me a while to recognise that. She could dismiss me early on as an annoying twit of a nephew. Our satisfying adult relationship really began – not surprisingly, as it turned out – when I bought her a painting at Christie's she had said she could not afford. Homer was the subject, but she liked to imagine the figure was the blind Connaught poet Raftery, whom she adored and whose Irish verse she was translating into English. After that, she gradually began to treat me with a maternal mix of affection, attentiveness, intimacy and concern. That was despite my initial reaction to her literary friends.

CHAPTER 7

When I first went down for a visit to Coole Park, I found Augusta enthusiastically hosting a gathering of the Irish revivalists, Yeats and Douglas Hyde among them. Yeats's absurd spiritualism, combined with his and Hyde's madness for old Irish folkways and the Irish language, I found silly and somehow disreputable. If my aunt was beginning to act motherly toward me, I wanted to give her paternal advice that she was being had by the wrong sort. I know that some of her Anglo-Irish neighbours around Coole let her know their feeling that no Irish speaker such as Hyde could ever be a gentleman.

My first impression of these revivalists was as a gaggle of fusspot pseudohistorians who wanted desperately to believe in mystical olden days of poor but eloquent Paddies, trotting through bleary bogs reciting sentimental poetry. Yeats at first was a particular problem. He told Augusta at one point that I was only interested in whisking fine old paintings out of Irish country houses so I could make a fortune selling them on the London market, unconcerned about diluting Ireland's cultural heritage in the process. He changed his mind after seeing the lavish gifts of paintings I was making to the Dublin Municipal Gallery. But she had to convince him initially of my worthiness to be admitted even to the antechamber of the Irish movement.

It was when Augusta began to suspect that I could contribute to the movement in my own way – or perhaps it was mostly to obtain for her untutored nephew a respectable first job in the culture industry – she called on a friend of her late husband Sir William to help me find an apprentice position in a London art gallery. I like to think she saw in me then a weak glimmer of potential to follow in Sir William's footsteps. He had been a trustee of and donor to the National Gallery of Art in London. But if my aunt projected a possible connection between her husband and me, I believe it was the proximity of my death to her son Robert's that made me in her mind another of her unlikely heroes in the cause of Ireland.

Robert died only three years after me, in 1918. She told my friend Alec Martin in the wake of her double loss: 'Now it is for the dead I am living'. Whereas she cajoled Yeats into writing beautiful poems in Robert's memory, she took on the task of writing my biography herself after finding several prospective biographers unsatisfactory. Needless to say, I appreciate her high standards in this regard. She wrote my life story as she had that of her husband – with painstaking care and genuine affection. She understood me because she understood my entanglement with my paintings. She loved me in no small part because I wanted to give the paintings to Ireland. They were as much the subject of the biography as I was. Just look at what she called the book: *Hugh Lane's Life and Achievement, With Some Account of the Dublin Galleries.*

It was Ireland's ungracious, dilatory acceptance of my gift that led me to write her a despondent letter in 1915 from which she quotes in the biography: 'My early romantic notion of Ireland was got in my childhood in Galway, and I am now so completely disillusioned that I don't want to be reminded of those early happy days'. In that same mood that same year I drew up a will that left thirty-nine pictures to London rather than Dublin. Spite is a powerful emotion, and I indulged mine powerfully, I thought, with this decision. The fumbling grandees in Dublin who dithered endlessly over how to accept the pictures and an appropriate venue for their display well deserved it.

I quickly started to regret exercising it in this fashion. I wanted the people of Ireland to enjoy this art as I did, to be ennobled by it, despite the ignoble Dublin art establishment. So in 1915, I added a codicil to my will reversing my earlier direction, giving the paintings to Ireland. Alas, the codicil was never legally witnessed before I met my fate on the *Lusitania* later that year. This tragic oversight on my part would come to preoccupy much of my aunt Augusta's later life.

She wrote the stories and empowered the work of the men around her – her husband, me, her literary, artistic and political friends. What would Yeats have been without her? Not Yeats. She played to the male ego with unparalleled dexterity to wring the best out of it. And then where she had the chance, she shaped and interpreted its legacy to her own liking and Ireland's credit. My legacy, my gifts of paintings to the National Gallery of Ireland and the Dublin Municipal Gallery, would prove devilishly difficult for her to ensure.

She was instrumental to my appointment as Director of the former. I named her sole Trustee of my plan to give paintings to the latter. Lady Gregory found the unwitnessed codicil to my will stating this intention in my desk at the National Gallery after my death. Then she was off to the races, fighting with the English government over its moral obligation to respect my stated wish, even though not legally binding, to have my paintings displayed in Dublin. She wanted them – and I believe through them, me – for Ireland. She went so far as to persuade the Irish leader Michael Collins to raise the return of my pictures from London to Dublin in the January 1922 negotiations with the British over the implementation of the treaty after the Anglo-Irish War.

That she did not manage to get the paintings back to Ireland in her lifetime, notwithstanding her ceaseless, uncompromising efforts to do so, I know disturbed what should have been a more peaceful and honoured set of senior years. She wrote in her diary upon seeing the Sargent portrait of me: 'The eyes seemed to follow me, seemed to reproach me for not having carried out what he had entrusted me to do, the bringing back of the French pictures to Dublin'. It was not until the 1950s, long after Lady Gregory's death in 1932, when the English decided they had garnered enough Impressionist paintings from other bequests to fill out their holdings in this genre, that they considered a sharing arrangement between London and Dublin.

The staffer charged by the British Prime Minister Harold Macmillan at the time with investigating such an arrangement wrote: 'It is questionable whether a compromise would ever satisfy the Irish, feeling as strongly as they do. Is it not better to leave the pictures where they belong and where they are valued, and to leave the Irish with their grievance, which they enjoy?' Unstinting in his smarmy superiority, don't you think? Nonetheless, the two nations finally agreed in 1959 to divide the collection in half and swap them every five years for display in both nations' capitals. The swapping and sniping continue to the present day, as Brexit could redefine such cross-border settlements.

Yet I know my aunt would be thrilled with the 1975 renaming of the Dublin Municipal Gallery to the Hugh Lane Municipal Gallery of Modern Art. Without all her desperate efforts to reclaim my 'French pictures', as she called them, for Ireland's cultural patrimony, I'm sure this recognition would not have happened. 'Patrimony' is perhaps the appropriate word here. For in those efforts, she gave so much of herself to make the reputation of yet another needy Irishman.

When the Dublin Municipal Gallery first opened in 1933, the year after her death, a room was set aside in a hopeful gesture to contain my paintings, which alas would not arrive until decades later. It stood vacant except for a single item – my friend Richard Orpen's bust of me. It was Lady Gregory who drew me into the middle of the Irish cultural revival, and eventually – as if from beyond the grave – filled that lonely room with the beauty I had gathered together. I am forever in her thrall.

Figure 8. Maire Nic Shiubhlaigh. Courtesy of the Abbey Theatre Archive.

CHAPTER 8

Maire Nic Shiubhlaigh (Mary Elizabeth Walker) 1883–1958

Maire Nic Shiubhlaigh was born Mary Elizabeth Walker but took an Irish form of her given name as a stage name. As a young, middle-class, nationalistic, Irish Catholic actress at the Abbey Theatre, her perspective on the Protestant, aristocratic Lady Gregory was from a sceptical distance. To Maire's young self then, Augusta seemed an odd old lady from Galway bossing the Dublin theatre folk around. But later Augusta would take her side in disputes with the supercilious Yeats. Like John Quinn, her admiration for Lady Gregory grew during the Abbey's 1911–2 American tour, when she saw the older woman stand up defiantly in the face of the rioters trying to shut down the 'immodest' performances. She was an active participant in the Easter 1916 Rising, joining the contingent of Irish rebels at Jacob's Biscuit and Cake Factory, even firing an errant shot from its roof. Over time she saw Augusta's attitude toward the rebellion changing, gradually becoming more sympathetic to the cause. When Augusta stepped in for Maire in the role of Cathleen Ni Houlihan one evening when she was late getting to the Abbey, however … well that was entirely beyond the pale!

I was born Mary Elizabeth Walker. But I was the first Irish actress to take an Irish form of my given name as a stage name. How is that now for fooling the Sassenach? I always loved words. I loved the sound of them, and the voice's interpretation of them. I suppose that's why I always wanted to be an actress.

I had only a small role in that first production of Yeats's *Cathleen Ni Houlihan* in 1902. Maud Gonne, with her rich golden hair, her pale, sensitive face and burning eyes, played – or rather *became* – that poor old woman as she spoke her closing lines about the young men who would fight and die for Ireland:

> They shall be remembered forever,
> They shall be alive forever,
> They shall be speaking forever,
> The people shall hear them forever […].

Yeats wrote the play especially for her. I thought she was the most beautiful woman I had ever seen. And she was one of us.

She set the audience vibrating with enthusiasm and quick to seize every point. The country was captivated by her, prideful in its belief that a small island that had produced this dramatic avatar of defiance could throw off its captivity to England. From that boxed-in, tiny stage at St Teresa's Hall she projected all the untamed energy of our wide national hopes and dreams.

It was backstage after Maud's nearly reckless performance that I first laid eyes on Lady Augusta Gregory. She was congratulating the actors, but her quiet condescension made her compliments feel awkwardly backhanded. Earnest in her way with her little lisping voice and odd accent, she became fully engaged with Frank and Willy Fay, throwing out ideas to improve the production they had worked so hard to craft. A curious old lady she seemed to my young self then, a sort of invigilator from the west of Ireland and the English aristocracy telling us Dublin Jackeens how to put on a play in the Irish capital city. It occurred to me later that if any one moment was, this was the moment when the movement that led to the Abbey Theatre was sparked – and Lady Gregory was already trying at once to fan the flames and control the fire.

But for all that, she and Yeats – with the prodding of the Fays – finally recognised that their Irish Literary Theatre had failed in no small part because the English actors they employed could not capture the Irish idiom that was the lifeblood of the new nationalistic dramas. It was the Irish amateur actors like myself, speaking in our natural voices on the stage, who built a house of words where the spirit of the nation might live again. The Fay brothers worked ceaselessly with all of us on voice and speaking style. When the Abbey had its opening night on 17 December 1904, I was ready to step into the role that Maud Gonne had so brilliantly originated two years earlier. Leading lady, playing Cathleen Ni Houilihan for the first time on the Abbey Theatre's first night. At twenty-one years old, I was embodying my country's sad history and high expectations.

My family was there not just to bask in the glory of it, but as the ground troops that made this Irish dramatic army function. My brother Frank was with me on stage in a minor role. Two of my sisters, Annie and Gypsy, sold programmes in the auditorium. My mother, Mary Anne, served as the wardrobe mistress, and my father, Matt, printed the programmes for the new National Irish Theatre Society. The Abbey was a way for our whole family to express our love of country, to 'act it out', if you will.

The family connection to the Abbey goes directly back to my parents' rabid support of Charles Stewart Parnell. My father accompanied Parnell on one of his last campaigns. It was in Kilkenny, I think – the time when an anti-Parnellite threw quicklime into the great man's eyes. My father attempted to shield Parnell's face with his hat, and the lime sprayed over it. Years later, my sister Gypsy and I were sitting at our kitchen table sewing costumes for an Abbey production. We needed a kind of tramp's hat, so we had taken an old one from the top of father's wardrobe and cut a proper hole in the top of it.

When he walked in on us his chin immediately slid to the floor, leaving a gaping hole in his face to match that of the hat. 'What is it? What is it?' I cried. 'Sure it was an old damaged thing sitting there up high that you never wore'. When he told us it was the very hat he had held over Parnell's eyes, we were destroyed. But kindly, dear man that he was, he recovered quickly and said to us calmly: 'No, don't apologise. That hat played a part in Irish history twelve years ago. It's playing its final act today'. I never think of my father without thinking of that story. It was as if Parnell was to see us through his damaged eyes and father's crownless hat fulfilling his dreams for a new Ireland in the new twentieth century.

But the Abbey Theatre never quite lived up to that billing. The Abbey for us was what some of my girlfriends said of men: 'You can't live with them and you can't live without them'. My generation came to the theatre fed up with the self-defeating bickering of parliamentarians, of Parnellites and anti-Parnellites. We saw it as an alternative venue for nationalist expression, unconstrained by political limitations with their inevitability of compromise. The theatre for us was always a means, not an end in itself. The end was always Irish freedom. So in that sense, I suppose we did use the stage as a political vehicle. We loved it nonetheless for all that. But for Lady Gregory and Yeats, well, they loved it because it was not that, it was 'art'.

All the Abbey's self-appointed leaders then were uppity Anglo-Irish or English Protestants – Yeats, Lady Gregory, certainly our heiress funder, Annie Horniman, even that lovely man John Synge who wanted to make art out of Ireland, not Ireland out of art. We were the working-class Catholic Irish boys and girls, with our commitments to nationalism, even to socialism and our own kind of feminism, who made their fairies and fools ring relevant to Irish audiences. On each side of the chasm of politics, class and religion, we understood we each had our own set of talents and experiences that conflicted with and complemented each other, neither sustaining art or nation on its own.

The chasm, though, was deep and wide. Yeats called me and the other actresses 'shop girls'. And what of it if we were? Wasn't he descended from nothing more than fancy merchants himself? He actually told Synge that women of my class did not have 'sensitive bodies'. As if he'd know. I wonder what Maud Gonne would have made of that stupid, snotty nonsense. When in 1905 they restructured the Irish National Theatre Society so that the Abbey was controlled entirely by Yeats, Lady Gregory and Synge, I'd had enough. They were blunt about what they were doing. Yeats called it 'an end to democracy in the theatre'. There would be no more cooperative decision-making by the entire company about what went on the stage and how it was played. We would take a rich Englishwoman's – Annie Horniman's – money to pay actors. They wanted to 'professionalise' us. The Abbey would no longer be part of a nationalist movement, but rather a producer of paid performances for aesthetes.

Not for me, it wouldn't. When I resisted Yeats's pressure to sign a new contract, he turned vicious, demeaning, and threatened to sue me. It got so bad that his father, J. B., and his sisters Lily and Lolly, felt compelled to take my side. L and L told Lady Gregory that their brother's 'sneery and offensive' treatment of me was unacceptable. Their father (I think he was a little in love with me – why else did he have me sit endlessly for those two beautiful portraits?) called his son a 'mad poet' in the 'hands of vulgar intriguers'.

W. B. tried to buy me off by offering me a role as a wardrobe mistress, like my mother, in addition to the actor's salary he said he would pay me. But I knew he was paying my rival Sara Allgood more, conniver that he was. Even in his Nobel Prize acceptance speech many years later he could not bring himself to be gracious. He called Allgood and another Abbey actress, Maire O'Neill, 'players of genius', with nary a mention of me.

Synge tried desperately to get me to stay with the Abbey. He used to make his own cigarettes. He would come around in the wings and offer to make them for me. He knew I had picked up a serious smoking habit in those wings, so he promised to give me my own cigarette-rolling machine if I would stay on. He could be thoughtful like that. Lady Gregory and he teamed up to stand Yeats down about suing me for breach of contract, telling him very directly they would not support any such absurdity. Augusta was solicitous in other ways as well that surprised me.

Although I sometimes thought of her as overbearing, she spoke to me in the middle of the row with Yeats and lifted my spirits a bit. When I decided in 1905 I did have to leave the company because I felt it had become more of a business enterprise than a platform for Irish identity, she asked me to stay until year's close to give her time to try to replace me. Miss Horniman had arranged a short English tour for the Abbey players, and my name was all over the advance publicity, so my leaving before the end of the year would wreck the anticipation in England. I agreed to stay that long and only that long.

I suppose I recognised at some level that to be successful the Abbey had to be more than an instrument of nationalism, and perhaps that was part of the reason I acceded to Lady Gregory's sensible request. Of course, I was flattered too to have her think me essential for the English tour. God help me, but I found the English audiences more appreciative than the Irish ones. Then in 1910, when Augusta was planning an American tour for the Abbey, she asked me to rejoin the company. She was again solicitous and persuasive, and the steady salary she offered to do what I loved most in the world convinced me at that point in my life that acting could indeed be my profession, not just my calling.

When I first came back into the fold, neither she nor I had it in mind that I would go with the original company to perform in America. But when Maire O'Neill became ill, I was chosen to take her place with only three days to pack for the theatrical odyssey that would take us halfway across the United States. On 12 September 1911, sixteen Abbey stalwarts and I set sail for Boston.

After a short while Yeats, who was with us managing things in America, left to return to Dublin, and Lady Gregory came over to lead us through the rest of the tour. As it turned out, that required more courage than any of us would have wished. We departed Boston in mid-November for New York. Our venue there was to be the off-Broadway Maxine Elliott Theatre. Augusta was so thoughtful as to outfit a small dressing room with books and periodicals for us. It became a kind of pleasant common room for the entire company, one that later took on the feel of a war room as we hunkered down to strategise over the 'reception' – if that's what you want to call it – of Synge's *The Playboy of the Western World*.

The first night we put on *Playboy* it started calmly enough. As soon as the Christy Mahon character made his entrance, however, the coughing, then murmuring, then hissing came at us. At first it sounded like Mass, with the congregants' catarrh interspersed with their quiet praying. But the volume rose quickly. Our voices on stage were nearly drowned out. Stomping and shouting, louder and louder. A woman's scream here and there. Then it began. It was if all the noise were cannons booming, firing the missiles that landed on stage. The cannon balls fired at us consisted of rolled-up balls of paper, pieces of sticks, a variety of not very fresh vegetables, half loaves of bread, well-ripened cabbages and a shower of big knobby potatoes, heavy, dusty and hard. Imagine. The louts.

Lady Gregory would have none of it. She shouted, 'Keep playing' from the wing, and then the house lights suddenly came on. The police stormed in, and it was hand-to-hand combat with the protesters. The curtain was lowered on the fighting festivities in the gallery, and Augusta appeared like a calm but powerful angel telling us to 'keep our heads'. Indeed, a few heads had taken a spud to the temple. But she assured us the police would get everything under control.

Moreover, she insisted that when the police had restored order, the entire first act would be played again. And so it was. And so was the whole *Playboy* performed that night. And so it was for the planned run of four nights. This odd little old lady was not to be deterred. If she had to stand up to a mob of raving hooligans to defend Irish art, she would.

The night after the opening night riot, Augusta invited former President Theodore Roosevelt to join her in her box. He attracted a standing cheer and enthusiastic applause when he entered. Acknowledging it briefly, he took Lady Gregory's hand and graciously moved her to the fore to share in the admiration. She had established her own bully pulpit with her behaviour the night before, and the ex-president knew a fearless fighter when he saw one. He later thrilled us by asking to be taken backstage to meet the company. He greeted us each personally, congratulating us on our performance and our courage. His eyes rested on Lady Gregory when he mentioned courage.

Then on to Philadelphia, where not only were rioters arrested, but we actors as well. Or at least we were technically 'under arrest' for violating a city law prohibiting the production of plays that might be judged as 'immodest'. One of our accusers asserted that *Playboy* was indeed 'immoral, indecent and sacrilegious', no doubt piling on most of the naughty adjectives he knew. These lame legal maneuverers withheld the issuing of the arrest warrants until a few minutes before the curtain was to rise on the first showing of *Playboy*, hoping to prevent it from going on.

But the redoubtable Lady Gregory, having sniffed out their pathetic plot, outmanoeuvred them. She had arranged for bail-bonds of $500 for each of us actors – I have no idea how or where she got the money – and the play went on that night. Our trial the next day was a sillier show than any comedy Augusta ever wrote, but with worrisome possible consequences. To paraphrase Samuel Johnson, the prospect of hanging greatly concentrates the mind. Perhaps the prospect of being stuck in jail in Philadelphia even more so.

There was no real likelihood of that, however, once Augusta's friend and lawyer from New York, John Quinn, showed up in Philadelphia to defend us. He was brilliant, with a stage presence I envied, and I had the sense he was performing in court for Augusta as much as for the righteous cause of Irish art. The older of the two, she seemed buoyed by his energy and articulateness. He was admiring and attentive with her. I guess there was something to those rumours. Well, more power to her. She did better than the rest of us in acquiring an American beau.

Be all that as it may, Quinn took over our defence midway through the trial and immediately started carving up the smarmy moralists who paraded through the pathetic case the prosecutor tried to make. One of the prosecution witnesses, for instance, claimed that the very fact that Christy and Pegeen were left alone in a room in one scene of *Playboy* spelled immorality. Quinn asked, 'Did anything take place on the stage to make you say that?' The witness responded no, 'it wasn't anything that went on on the stage'. He hesitated, and then added, 'But we all know what happened when the curtain fell'.

Most of the proceeding went on like that, and five or six days later we learned that the case had been dismissed. In fact, it helped draw new and appreciative playgoers during our run in Philadelphia. It was Lady Gregory's wily persistence in the face of thrown objects, lawsuits, even personal death threats that kept us all focused on and committed to showing our American cousins that little Ireland had a culture that could move the world. I never forgot that about her, even after it was time to move from culture to arms and leave her behind.

The call to rebellion was literally a family matter in my case. On Easter Monday morning 1916 I was attending Mass. My father arrived at the church breathless and slipped me a telegram. It was from my comrade and friend Lily Brennan. It said, 'Come at once'. Imagine a father who would carry the message into church summoning his daughter into harm's way in a violent revolution. He loved me and loved Ireland and believed his daughters should play their role in the drama of national creation, whatever sacrifices that might require. And so I went.

It was almost like a grand opening night for us. So many of the plays in our repertoire were, in effect, rehearsals for revolution. Lady Gregory told me that George Bernard Shaw said to her that after seeing the London performance of *Cathleen Ni Houlihan* he feared it might lead a man to do something foolish. Indeed, at the start of the Easter Rising some in Dublin mistook it for improvised street theatre. One critic even thought the Proclamation of the Republic was a playbill. The *Daily Chronicle's* correspondent wrote, right after the rebellion as the leaders were being executed by firing squad: 'Has not this revolution in some sense a genesis in the Irish Theatre?'

The Abbey was a kind of mother to the Rising. Two of its founders signed the Proclamation. Many of my Abbey friends joined me on the Easter Monday ramparts. Our fine young actor Sean Connelly, with a wife and three young children, killed a constable and then was shot through the stomach himself, bleeding to death on the roof of Dublin City Hall. The only one of us to die in the fighting, he had been hit by a sniper from the Dublin Castle clock tower.

When I heard that the rebels had taken Jacob's Biscuit and Cake Factory in Bishop Street, I made my way there. I guess the culinary business of the place was appropriate for the women who joined that garrison – we had six, all under twenty except for me at thirty-three, and it was made clear we were there to cook for the men. But at one point I climbed the tower at Jacob's to get a hot chocolate to one of our snipers. He handed me his rifle so he could grab the mug. I raised it and fired a round into the air. When he angrily admonished me for wasting bullets, I just told him I always wanted to fire a shot in an Irish rebellion, as long as I didn't have to kill anybody.

We at Jacob's fared better than the women who wanted to join the boys at Boland's Mill. There, the prissy commander Eamon de Valera, eventually Prime Minister and later President of Ireland, refused to let them enter and sent them home. Some went to other rebel-held sites and were welcomed. I heard that De Valera said years later, sheepishly, that he had lost the fighting services of some good men who had to cook in the place of the females he had insultingly dismissed. So much for dedication to the 'equal rights and equal opportunities of all its citizens', declared in the Proclamation of the Irish Republic read out by Patrick Pearse in front of the General Post Office at the start of the Rising.

Despite the patriotic pigheadedness on the part of some of the men, we women did what we could to strike a blow for Ireland. I think of Nellie Bushell, who began working as an usherette at the 1904 opening of the Abbey at age sixteen, and continued in that role until her death in 1948. The local historian Seamus Scully, to whom she gave a pass to the cheap seats, described her on opening night outfitted in Lady Gregory's favourite uniform:

> Daintily clad in black frock and skirt, fronted by white-laced apron, dark stockings and shoes, which Lady Gregory had asserted was the most graceful attire for the Abbey usherettes, she was a dignified figure as she guided patrons down the few parterre steps to their seats, and courteously presented them with the buff-grey coloured programme.

By the time of the Anglo-Irish War in the early 1920s, this same epitome of feminine modesty, politeness and culture served as a sophisticated gunrunner. Nellie would hide the Irish rebels' guns, ammunition and explosives in the Abbey library. She checked guns at the door for Michael Collins and his men when they would attend a play, and once smuggled him out of the Abbey with the Black and Tan British goons in hot pursuit. She was said to have enough gelignite stored in the Abbey library to blow the whole place sky high. Lady Gregory never caught a whiff of it (indeed, if she had, it would have been too late), and was always pleased with Nellie's demure dress and manner.

I suppose it was a miracle of sorts that the Abbey was not blown apart in the 1916 fighting that so tore up Dublin. Many other buildings and businesses on Lower and Middle Abbey Street were destroyed. Augusta wrote to Yeats that 'bricks from burning buildings fell even on the steps'. Abbey manager St John Ervine reported only a broken lamp outside the stage door and a few shattered panes of glass outside the pit door. Mr Ervine was an Irish West Briton, hated everything about the Rising, and even referred to De Valera as that 'damned dago!'

We were all worried about whether the Abbey could survive in the aftermath, with so much of the neighbourhood and indeed the city's infrastructure in ruins. As late as his Nobel acceptance speech, Yeats remarked: 'audiences grow thin when there is firing in the streets'. He and Augusta had a difficult time making sense of what the Rising meant for the Abbey and the country.

Augusta always had a particular admiration, even affection, for the tragic Sean Connolly I mentioned earlier. Not only was he the sole Abbey player killed in the 1916 fighting – I believe he was the first Irishman to die in the conflict. On her way home to Galway on a train in 1921, after the death of her son, Robert, in the First World War, Augusta wrote on the back of a letter: 'What led you to those castle walls? We mourn you Sean Connolly'. She knew too well the price young men – and their families – paid in war. She loved what she called Sean's 'beautiful and distinguished work' in her play, *Kincora*. Yeats wrote that he 'might have been/a famous, a brilliant figure/Before the painted scene'.

They seemed to feel a mix of regret, disappointment, and confusion. Right after the Rising, Augusta had petulantly expressed to Yeats her opposition to it: 'One has no pity for those who know what the Germans have done in Belgium and want to bring them into Ireland and who have taken German money'. She had been isolated at Coole Park during Easter Week, brooding in Galway on rumours and reports of the violence in Dublin. As the impact of the swift executions of Pearse and all the other leaders came home, her tone shifted. In another note to Yeats, paying homage to the rebels but still with more than a hint of Ascendancy condescension, she wrote: 'it seems as if the leaders were what is wanted in Ireland – and will be even more wanted in the future – a fearless and imaginative opposition to the conventional and opportunistic parliamentarians, who have never helped our work'.

What did she think, that the likes of Pearse and MacDonagh were some sort of intellectual bohemians? She thought she should have brought them over to 'our side', as she put it to Yeats. But their upper crust Ascendancy crowd was tone deaf to the passionate song of Irish freedom that needed fearless singing – and would propel fearless action – beyond their pretty plays and poems. In his poem, 'Man and the Echo', alluding to *Cathleen Ni Houlihan*, Yeats boastfully wonders:

> Did that play of mine send out
> Certain men the English shot?

Despite what George Bernard Shaw or Yeats might think, the answer to Yeats's question is definitely not. It was rather 800 years of brutal English suppression in

CHAPTER 8

Ireland that did it. The man and the echo indeed. Willie Yeats spent a lot of time echoing himself. So much so that your contemporary Irish poet Paul Muldoon could not resist his own sharp echo:

> If Yeats had saved his pencil lead
> Would certain men have stayed in bed?

Again, definitely not.

Just as Yeats and Augusta had a hard time knowing what to make of Easter 1916, I still have a hard time knowing what to make of her. She was a small, not very striking, middle-aged woman when I first met her in 1902. She would square up the shoulders on her bulky figure and patrol the Abbey in her strutting walk. She had a tight, thin-lipped, fixed social smile, and talked rapidly in her odd, flat-toned way. She was a combination of understanding aunt, hospitable hostess and imperious taskmistress.

One evening when I was delayed getting to the Abbey for an appearance as Cathleen Ni Houlihan, she horrified Yeats and the company by stepping into the part herself. Think of the immense, misguided bravado of the woman. If we could only see ourselves as others see us. She managed to deliver Yeats's beautiful, inspiring lines in a manner somehow simultaneously flat and sing-songy. At this point in her life, she should never have dreamed of answering a casting call to play Cathleen Ni Houlihan. Nevertheless, she always spoke of her turn as my understudy with a naïve pride and satisfaction as the realisation of a lifelong ambition.

I suppose at some level she wanted to be the female incarnation of Irish cultural nationalism. Earlier I mentioned the women De Valera had sent home. Lady Gregory would never be sent home by any man from her cause of building Irish identity as she saw it. I suppose in that we are more alike than not.

Figure 9. Robert Gregory. Courtesy of Colin Smythe.

CHAPTER 9

Robert Gregory 1881–1918

Robert Gregory was the only child of Augusta and her husband, Sir William Gregory. Killed while flying in the RAF over Italy in World War I, he became an iconic presence in Ireland's literary landscape by virtue of Yeats eulogising him in the poems, 'An Irish Airman Foresees His Death' and 'In Memory of Major Robert Gregory'. As a boy he loved the outdoor freedom of his home at Coole Park, playing cricket on the front lawn and horseback riding across its fields. As he got older, the responsibilities of overseeing the estate wore on him, and his cosmopolitan wife, Margaret, was less than comfortable at her mother-in-law's remote demesne. Both artists, Robert and she pursued their careers and enjoyed their Bohemian friends in London and Paris. Their three children found themselves spending much time, happily, at Coole with their grandmother. A messy extramarital affair, and his own feeling that he was a kind of grand poseur, master of nothing really important in life, set the stage for his escape into a war where he believed he could prove his worth. Uncomfortable with his mother's Irish literary circle and no Irish nationalist, he would die defending the British Empire about which his mother and Yeats had increasing doubts.

Those galoshes. My mother walking in them with my little daughters, Anne and Catherine, across the fields of Coole Park, thrusting at weeds with her spade. The girls sprinting, screaming, smelling the wet soil and hearing the protestations of the birds they happily disturbed, delighted with their man-booted grandmother's ferocious management of their home grounds' untoward invaders. Her way of showing them what it is like for a Lady to love the very dirt of her demesne, under foot and fingernail. They well absorbed these lessons about their father's birthplace.

My mother taught them the finer points of estate management as well. The setting was high tea at the Standard Hotel in Dublin. As Anne tells it, when they finished their grandmother drew an envelope from her purse and tipped into it all the sugar from the sugar bowl on the table. She then returned the envelope to her purse. Catherine – or Nu as she was called in the family – asked her grandmother why she had done that. The Lady explained that she paid for the sugar but never used it in her tea, so did not see why she should leave it for the Standard Hotel to sell to somebody else.

My mother embarrassed the girls by performing this sleight of hand regularly. By the girls' account this was the only quirk of their grandmother that embarrassed them. For she lovingly looked after their health, their social development, their education – as she did with my son, Richard – while giving them rein to run about the four corners of Coole. She took on the role of their governess after dismissing one she judged incompetent. That while my wife, Margaret, and I were often vacationing at the house in the Burren my mother bought for us, or tending to our art careers in Paris or London.

My mother was always companionable with children. She was so with me, at least when I got old enough to function as companion to her. She taught me croquet and took me on many outings. In London we went skating in St James Park and visited the National Gallery and the House of Commons. She explained my father's service as a trustee of the Gallery and as a Conservative member for Dublin and later for Galway in the House of Commons. She brought me along to a different sort of house, the Gort Workhouse, to distribute fruit to the children. My mother was keen to have me come to terms with our obligations to our Coole Park tenants and the poor. She also wanted me to understand them, how and why the Irish Catholics were different from us.

When I expressed interest in learning Irish at age sixteen – a cultural and linguistic pursuit to complement my preoccupations with cycling, boating, boxing and cricket – she was thrilled and made it a mother-and-son effort. Alas my introduction to partridge shooting later that year greatly slackened my commitment to studying Irish. She went on with it on her own, developing over time a fair proficiency with the help of one of our tenants. So I like to proclaim that I am the person responsible for Lady Augusta Gregory knowing something about the language that moulded the native Irish culture she helped make famous throughout the world.

But I know now our closeness was not there from the start. My mother never recorded my christening in her diary and wrote little about me as a baby in her letters. My father was even less enthusiastic. Grumpy about the new demands an infant placed on his young wife and their marriage, he wrote to my godfather, Henry Layard: 'I wish to heavens he could be shut up […] till he reaches the age of seven *at least*'. This after he told Layard while my mother was pregnant: 'People congratulate me on the prospect of being a father which I dread and detest. My wife is so poorly that she cannot do anything at present so as I am likely to be detained at Coole much longer than I intended. I have left her there with her sister and come up to London'.

They dropped me off when I was only two months old at my grandmother Persse's house in Dublin so they could troop off to the Continent for a month-long tour of Belgium, Holland and Germany. Later in the year of my birth they were off to Egypt. There my mother would play the Egyptologist and fall in hero love with the Egyptian nationalist Arabi Bey, and real love with the scoundrel Wilfrid Scawen Blunt. She, the newlywed, conducted her heedless affair with Blunt right under my father's old, dysfunctional nose.

Were these escapes driven by a first-time mother's uncertainly about care of infants, along with her husband's hotly reiterated reluctance to have their freedoms curtailed in any way? Or was it something else?

I have been troubled by the persistent Gort legend that my biological father was not the sixty-four-year-old Sir William, but the young Coole blacksmith Seanin Farrell. The rumour the local people loved to spread was that Farrell had been approached to perform this service and then spirited away to America for good and all. They said I had his small stature and sharpish features. My mother never breathed a word of this to me, of course. But I noticed in her diary entries after my father died that 'old Farrell', Seanin's father, attracted a disproportionate amount of attention. I'll never know the truth of it. However I came into this world, Lady Gregory had given birth to the heir of Coole, thereby greatly enhancing her stature on the Anglo-Irish landscape.

Coole for me was a mixed blessing. As a child I loved it there, as did my own young children. The woods, the water, the animals, the wildness of the place. When I was at boarding school in London, I longed for it. I attacked every outdoor sport on its grounds a young man could. I involved the tenants and employees in all that, captaining our cricket team on the front lawn. Quite the aspiring country gentleman. But as I grew older, the responsibilities of maintaining the fields and the house, as well as Coole's remoteness from the centre of things in London and Paris, began to pinch. I tried to be the dutiful heir, but my mother animated the place, bringing all there under her unbending sway. It could feel claustrophobic.

That's why my wife, Margaret, and I spent so much time in the English and French capitals, as I mentioned, lived our cosmopolitan lives, pursuing our careers in art and enjoying the friends in our rather Bohemian circle. Even the house on the Galway coast my mother gave us became a haven to escape to with our English and French colleagues.

She had named it Mount Vernon in homage to George Washington, progenitor of American freedom. I thought the name an ironic symbol of our freedom from Coole. While Margaret and I lived our very international lives, the children spent more and more time with their grandmother at Coole. I suppose I should not ruminate too much about absentee parents. The Irish complained enough about absentee landlords.

Despite sentimental connections, I set my mind to sell Coole in 1909. Having 'come of age' on my twenty-first birthday in 1902, I was legally its owner. The Land Act of 1909 was pushing Anglo-Irish landlords to sell property to their tenants or to the government. We sold some parcels to tenants, but I decided to put the whole place up for sale and be done with it. We could not get a fair price for the estate, though, at the same time that the tenants were being gifted rent reductions by the Land Courts. More and more the place felt like an albatross hung around my neck.

But I knew my mother was quietly relieved that she would not have to build a new life away from Coole Park. We still owned it when I was killed in World War I in 1918, and indeed my mother would live there the rest of her life, with my wife Margaret's often annoyed acquiescence. More about that later. An incident vividly recalled by my daughter Anne that occurred at Coole during the Irish Civil War, after my death, sums up my ambivalence toward it.

Anne and my other daughter, Nu, were chasing a rabbit in the woods when they came upon two men with rifles. Recognising the girls, the men insisted on escorting them out of the woods and walking them up to the house garden. They told the girls not to come back to the woods for at least three days, since there were a lot of men on the run coming through. When they arrived back at the house, they told my mother that one of the men had said: 'Tell her Ladyship that we wouldn't hurt a hair of anyone in Her Ladyship's family'. Upon hearing this my mother teared up, but she told my daughters she had a cold coming on and it always made her nose and eyes run very fast. So the youngest generation of the Gregory family avoids injury or death only by virtue of a pass their grandmother has earned for championing Irish culture. Coole and country don't really feel much like an embracing homeland for the Gregorys, do they?

On 15 May 1921, my wife, Margaret, had her own 'hundred thousand welcomes' experience in the midst of the Anglo-Irish War. On this Sunday afternoon she had motored with some friends the short trip from Coole Park to Ballyturin House, the home of the Bagots, for an afternoon of tennis. She said later that it struck her as odd that on a fine Sunday afternoon they saw nobody out along the way. Her companions in the motorcar were Royal Irish Constabulary District Inspector Blake, Mrs Blake, and two military officers.

After their tennis matches and a bit of socialising, they left the house at about 8:30 PM. The car wound down the long avenue of the property, and as they approached the gate, they saw it was closed. One of the military men got out to open it. The first shot rang out. A group of some ten IRA men ordered the ladies to leave. Mrs Blake responded sharply that she would never leave her husband but die by his side if it came to that. And so it did. The IRA contingent fired volley after volley at close range, killing District Inspector Blake, Mrs Blake, and both military officers. Mrs Blake, who was said to be pregnant, was left with eight wounds, some from explosive bullets, several in her head.

When the firing stopped, Margaret was led back toward the house by some of the IRA men. They had clearly decided in advance she was not to be harmed. Hysterical and in shock, she was handed over to the younger Bagot daughter. She and her parents had run down toward the gate when they heard the shots. Her father was then handed a note by one of the IRA murderers that read: 'Volunteer HQ. Sir, if there are any reprisals after this ambush, your house will be set on fire as a return. By Order IRA'.

This appalling savagery was justified by stories that Blake had bullied the local population, threatening women with his revolver in the homes of wanted men, brandishing it freely in the shops in town, demanding to be served at once. Others insisted he was popular in the district and had travelled about freely. One's opinion no doubt dictated by one's tribal allegiance.

I'll grant that it came against the background of the brutality the Black and Tans and Auxiliaries had inflicted on the people of south Galway in the name of the Crown. It was claimed, for instance, that this particularly bloody crime was retaliation for an incident in which the paramilitaries had tortured three nationalists for information, forcing them to dig their own graves and threatening to bury them alive. At the same time, the IRA was pressuring the Bagots to sell off land on the Ballyturin estate, and they were resisting. In the long run the IRA got its way, for although the house was never burned, the family eventually left it to fall into total ruin.

Margaret never fully recovered from this horror. I was not there to help her through, having given my life in defence of the same Crown the Black and Tans so tarnished in Ireland. To make it much worse, there was the vicious lie of a rumour that my mother had conspired with the IRA to plan the attack, and that was why Margaret was the only one of the five spared. The following day my mother received a message from the IRA telling her she was safe 'as long as there was a Gregory in Coole'. Could you imagine a more perverse way to wonder for the rest of your life if you were wholly in debt to your mother-in-law for it?

Their relationship was a constantly shifting and reversing mess of appreciation, tenderness, resentment, and hostility. When Margaret and I were engaged in 1907, my mother wrote to her American friend John Quinn, describing Margaret as 'a very charming girl [...] clever, pretty and very bright and good. She is Welsh, with a Spanish grandmother, French great-grandmother and has no English blood, and that I am just as glad of'. Although admiring in tone, this judgement seems to me a bit like checking the horse's teeth to determine its fitness for service. My mother's relief in imagining her daughter-in-law-to-be might by blood have little interest in sympathising with British policy on Ireland was to be short-lived. Moreover, she shared with her confidante Yeats early on that she had 'a slight nervousness about the advent of Margaret, happy as I am about her, it must make a difference. I had been so free and unquestioned'.

Augusta did give me a beautiful sapphire for Margaret's engagement ring and bequeathed her some shares of Ceylon tea stock. I could sense my mother's uneasiness beneath the delight with the arrival of our firstborn, Richard, in 1909. The birth of the next generation male heir made her feel as though his mother had become mistress of Coole, and she shunted. The thwarted attempt to sell Coole that same year, which I knew my mother was more than ambivalent about, hardly helped to settle her down. They collaborated artistically nonetheless, with Margaret illustrating three of my mother's books for children. Our girls were born in 1911 and 1913. They seemed to give my mother some relief from her worries over being displaced at Coole, as she began to mother them there herself while Margaret and I sojourned in London and Paris.

My open affair with Nora Summers in 1915 drove a wedge not only between Margaret and me, but also between Augusta and me. She was so pathetically guilty about her affair with Wilfrid Scawen Blunt so early in her own marriage that she reacted very badly to my straying with Nora. She was particularly troubled by my unsuccessful efforts to have Margaret accept my new relationship. After all, Nora and her husband, Gerald, were friends of Margaret and me, part of our circle of fellow painters in London. Why couldn't we all accept the vagaries of the human heart like mature adults and live with their implications?

Alas, I wound up a party of one in my ease at doing that. Augusta told me I had made a right hames of things and she regretted having lived to see her son revealed a cad. She was so overwrought that she would not let me see her off at the station when she departed for her tour of America that year. If I was a cad, what in God's name was Blunt?! My one-year dalliance was indeed just that, ending with a violent quarrel with Nora and her husband. All that was part of the reason I shortly after made the otherwise patriotic decision to secure a commission with the Fourth Royal Connaught Rangers at the age of thirty-four, going off to defend the British Empire, leaving family matters behind for a war that would prove the end of me. My mother, in contrast, stayed close friends with Blunt for the rest of his scandalous life.

I wanted to be part of the air war. That premonition I had of a plane crashing beyond trees that were out behind a wall did not startle me. The life expectancy for new combat pilots was less than a month. I prepared a will that read, in its entirety: 'I wish to leave everything I have to my wife, Margaret Gregory. I wish her to have the fullest freedom in the upbringing of my children and the management of my house and estate'. It was made in haste, on a troop train, witnessed by two second lieutenants in my squadron. I felt I needed to make it clear that if anything happened to me, my mother should not interfere with how my wife wanted to raise the children and run the estate.

As it turns out, Margaret was not all that interested in either. She said she was afraid the children would marry peasants if they stayed at Coole. So both responsibilities defaulted to the older Lady of Coole, who retained the right to live there for the rest of her life. What was it Sean O'Casey called her – Blessed Brigid of Coole. There you had the perfect formula for the yet more intense conflict between mother-in-law and daughter-in-law that ensued after my death.

The support they gave each other that spilled almost into affection when I was killed soon dissipated. They developed their own little quiet, simmering, mutual ingratitude society. Margaret felt that my mother never paid her the respect she deserved for playing the indulgent absentee landlady for a time. My mother, in turn, working very hard under real financial constraints to keep the place in admirable condition to be turned over to our son, Richard, when the time came, believed Margaret to be distracted, irresponsible and selfish.

Increasingly, too, my mother wanted Coole preserved as a monument to the rejuvenation of Irish culture. She felt that all the work on that grand project accomplished there by her leading light guests and herself, and all the influence that work was having beyond Coole's borders, should be recognised as having been nurtured within its stately walls and on its carefully tended grounds. Was it not the most famous house in Ireland? Nevertheless, by 1920–1 Margaret was manoeuvring to sell Coole out from under Augusta. Yeats's sister Lily was outraged by her plotting, slamming her in a letter to John Quinn as 'Just a little suburban minx who has been to a school of art and gathered a little knowledge there'.

In 1926, my mother had her second operation for breast cancer. In the wake of that agony, some of the fight over ownership of Coole left her. In April 1927, Margaret sold what remined of Coole Park, house and lands, to the Forestry Commission, continuing the provision that Lady Augusta could occupy the house until her passing. Her annual rent payment was 100 pounds. After long years of considerable commitment to the welfare of her tenants, she had been reduced to the status of tenant herself.

Margaret used the proceeds to buy an historic country house she could make truly her own, Celbridge Abbey. In what certainly must have seemed to my mother the ultimate indignity, she agreed to Margaret's desire to take the library shelves from Coole for her new house. Margaret took some of the better furniture and the drapes from the drawing room as well. She was to marry my bold successor, Captain Guy Gough, from a strong unionist family, in 1928. They lived for a while at Celbridge, formerly the home of one of Jonathan Swift's love interests, Vanessa.

Gough's people were the sort who might have approved of eating the children of the Irish poor, as Swift so famously and satirically suggested in 'A Modest Proposal for Preventing the Children of Poor People from Being a Burthen to Their Parents or Country, and for Making Them Beneficial to the Publick'. I don't know that they would have recognised it as satire. Alright, this is a bit nasty of me toward my replacement in my wife's affections. But bloody hell, my mother gave away the bride at the wedding! The always sharp-tongued Lily Yeats thought that by the close of the ceremony Augusta looked fifteen years younger for having gotten rid of Margaret, more or less. She would live only four more years, however, dying at age eighty in 1932.

A few months later the remaining contents of the house at Coole were auctioned off, with Augustus John drawings and Jack Yeats paintings going for a few pounds. Yeats wrote in his diary: 'It will be before long an office and a residence for foresters, a little cheap furniture in the great rooms, a few religious oleographs its only pictures'. In 1991, the government sold the house to a building contractor. It was pulled down for the value of the stone. All the ignorant, small-minded, greedy forces released by the Irish revolution I'm sure took no pause over the dismantling.

Yeats understood us, the Anglo-Irish, the big house grandeur and all else Ireland was losing as it came into the hands of smaller-minded men. At first I liked him, and his brother even better. Jack, so much more relaxed and earthbound than the ethereal and theosophic W. B., would play cricket and ride with me when I was just old enough to do both. He even let me sketch with him as he worked on his paintings. His ease with his craft, and with me, was part of what made me want to be an artist myself. Could you ever imagine Willie on the back of a horse or swinging a cricket bat – or letting a young boy write with him on one of his poems? Nonetheless, I sided with him in his fights with his sisters over the quality of what was to be published by their Dun Emer Press.

He was right to be more demanding of their operations and publishing decisions. Their squabbles prompted his sister Lolly, as snippy a sibling as Lily, to write of W. B.: 'He has quarrelled with all his friends in Ireland (but Lady Gregory and the little mutual admiration society down there.)' Lolly thought my mother and the literary friends she gathered at Coole were an incestuous, self-serving lot. Not entirely wrong on that count, but Willie did try to be helpful to me now and again.

When my cousin, Hugh Lane, went down on the *Lusitania* and a new director for the Dublin Municipal Gallery needed to be appointed to replace him, Yeats pushed for my selection. He pushed hard. Now at the same time, mind you, he was calling me a directionless dilettante in his private notebook. Just like him to be so unashamedly two-faced. But I suppose his vocal advocacy for me is another testament to his deference to and regard for my mother. She of course had prompted him to speak up on my behalf. The effort proved fruitless. Even though he was always ambivalent about my talents and purposefulness, his frustration over his failed attempt to place me provoked one of his contemptuous broadsides against Mother Ireland. This in a letter to John Quinn: 'It is wonderful the amount of toil and intrigue one has to go through to accomplish anything in Ireland. Intelligence has no organisation whilst stupidity always has'.

Petty sarcasm from a fellow who spent so much time writing poems and plays to the Ireland in his head while living like a seigneur off our estate at Coole Park. When he first arrived at Coole as a young man only a few days after meeting my mother, she immediately ensconced him in a quiet, attractive room over the library with a clear view of the lake. She had laid thick rugs along the passageway on either side of his door to prevent even the sound of a floorboard creak from disturbing his poetic reveries.

As I grew older, I noticed he was stripping my father's wine cellar of its best vintages, with my mother's unrestrained encouragement. Finally, I had to ask him to bring his own wine and decanter when he came down to Coole. After I was gone, Margaret in her feisty widowhood would ask him to pay for his own food. Through it all, my mother took his side – even after she died! In a painful postmortem affront, her will left one of my paintings, hung in Yeats's room (as he thought of it), to him. It was as if she handed over a piece of my legacy to her spoilt darling.

She tried to put part of her own legacy in his control as well. In the last few years of her life, she asked him to find a publisher for her diaries, letters and autobiographical writings. She was afraid that if they fell into Margaret's hands after her death, her pro-British daughter-in-law would cut any references to England's depredations in Ireland. I think she overestimated Margaret's interest and capabilities in this regard. Nonetheless, here was another instance of Yeats intruding into family affairs.

Margaret certainly felt even before our marriage that there was far too much of that. When she first came to visit Coole, Yeats professed that she and I were 'fighting for mastery'. He enjoyed watching the match – as competition and

CHAPTER 9

flirtation – play out. She really did not want him around during her pregnancies, but he loomed. Even when he was not there, the house and grounds seemed to summon his spirit, as if we were perpetually caught up in one of his mad theosophical seances.

Our inability to be rid of him, and my mother's constant catering to him, led on occasion to nasty exchanges at the dinner table. Margaret's general attitude toward him became one of simmering sarcasm, roiled by his air of nosy entitlement. For his part, he convinced himself finally that her harrowing experience in the Ballyturin ambush, and her marriage into the unionist Gough family, had turned her irretrievably anti-republican, perhaps at base anti-Irish.

What brought them into a brief harmony was my mother's decline and passing. Margaret actually urged Yeats to spend all the time he could with her at Coole toward the end. He did so, but on a night he happened to be in Dublin, he received a call from my mother's solicitor that she was near death. He rushed to Coole the next morning. He was met at the station by our daughter Catherine, who told him that Lady Gregory had died just after midnight. He wept bitterly and uncontrollably. Margaret and I will give him that – he was a creature of my mother's making and loved her for it.

I am fully aware that she was the only reason Yeats wrote the poems about me. Indeed, until my Horatian 'Dulce et decorum est pro patria mori' death, there was not so much to celebrate about my life. I was an indifferent, idle schoolboy at Harrow. I knew I was a disappointment to the family, never achieving head of class status as my father and grandfather had. My mother fretted so about all that. I sensed she was crestfallen about my uneven art career as well, although she would not say it out loud.

She and Yeats both appreciated some of my minimalist set designs for their Abbey plays, but they groused that I held them back by painting too slowly. I pursued a gentleman's pursuits, achieving an admirable competence in horsemanship and cricket, and enjoying the role of benign landlord, although often an absentee one. Yet I did not feel I had risen to mastery of anything genuinely important in life. I believed myself to be mostly a repeat poseur, and worried that those who knew me well believed that too. Even as a young man, I felt as Yeats's old man in his 'Sailing to Byzantium' poem: 'but a paltry thing,/A tattered coat upon a stick'.

When the war gave me a chance to prove my worth as my life hung in the balance, I jumped at it. I could make my mark in defence of the British Empire that my mother and Yeats increasingly had doubts about, and I was glad of it. I was no Irish nationalist, no Sinn Feiner. They were the lobbish boyos rioting at the Abbey Theatre. To spite them all I became a decorated Irish RAF fighter pilot, earning the Military Cross for conspicuous gallantry and dedication to duty. My men in the 40 Squadron followed me without question, and the French adopted me with membership in their Legion d'Honneur.

After my plane went down, my mother all but forced Yeats to write his poems commemorating me. He complained in a letter to his wife about Augusta attempting, in effect, to ghostwrite 'In Memory of Major Robert Gregory':

> It has been a little thorny but we have settled a compromise. I have got from her a list of musical place-names where he has hunted… I have firmly resisted all suggested eloquence about aero planes 'and the blue Italian sky'. It is pathetic for Lady Gregory constantly says 'it is his monument – all that remains'.

They also conspired to raise my poetic tombstone in 'An Irish Airman Foresees His Death'. There Yeats puts words into my ghostly mouth: 'My country is Kiltartan Cross//My countrymen Kiltartan's poor'. That is misleading and far too simple. It reflects what my mother would have me be, not the discord of what I was. That was a Royal Air Force Anglo-Irish airman in His Majesty's service, neither fully Kiltartan-bound nor fully London-loyal.

Most of us Anglo-Irish were caught in this uneasy ethnic netherworld. Over time, through her work, hard-earned wisdom, and force of will, my mother transformed herself into a twentieth-century Irish patriot. In my short life, I never could. I never grew into the icon that she and Yeats portrayed after my death.

There was one damn Yeats poem my mother hated, 'Reprisals'. In it he has the temerity to call my ghost from my grave in Padua to return to Coole Park to fight my fellow Great War veterans who were wrecking bloody havoc on the local population during the Anglo-Irish War. They filled the ranks of the Black and Tans I mentioned earlier, sent to Ireland by the British government to retaliate against IRA members, their families and communities. Emblematic of that government's bottomless, brutal cynicism toward Ireland, the Conservative MP Hugh Gascoigne-Cecil said: 'There is no such thing as reprisals, but they are having a good effect'.

By the end of the poem the war-weary Yeats seems to have despaired of my intervention, urging my risen ghost back into the tomb: 'Then close your ears with dust and lie//Among the other cheated dead'. Who gave him the right to trouble my Italian sleep with a call to arms back in Ireland against my former comrades? His effrontery in manipulating my image and my family for his own poetic and political purposes was shameful.

Yet one thing Yeats got correct in 'Reprisals' was that I died a happy warrior. Although he exaggerated a modest bit in attributing to me nineteen German planes brought down, I was a skilled and deadly combat pilot. That was why there

CHAPTER 9

was such hubbub about precisely how I died. Killed in action, friendly fire, some other explanation? The military report says that my Sopwith F.1 Camel was last seen at 610 metres when it went into a spin and crashed. The official cause was listed as 'unknown'. But of course, I know.

I had taken anti-typhoid medication. The doctors warned us pilots that it could cause lightheadedness, dizziness, disorientation. But I had to fly. I wanted to get my kill number up. The doctors were right. I tried to fight off the drowsiness, gradually losing control, and then I plummeted. Here's the irony. The vaccine was developed at Trinity College and saved thousands of lives in the war that ended mine. An Anglo-Irishman in a British plane in a British war accidently killed by a wonder drug based on research done at the great Anglo-Protestant college in Dublin.

I lie now not uncomfortably in my Paduan grave. St Anthony of Padua is the patron saint of lost articles, lost people. While among the living I was always lost between England and Ireland. In my death I became a vivid symbol of all the sons lost in the Great War. My mother could never bring herself to visit my gravesite in Padua, whether out of overwhelming grief or unacknowledged disappointment.

Figure 10. Lady Gregory later in life. Courtesy of Colin Smythe.

CHAPTER 10

Lady Augusta Gregory *Vale* 1852–1932

There is no need to reintroduce here the Lady Gregory whose ghostly voice is heard in this final chapter. The reader met her in the preface and the first chapter and has become more and more familiar with her from a variety of perspectives as the other ghosts in this book have had their say about her. In this last chapter, the farther reaches of memory and foresight preoccupy her as she comes to grips with the long trajectory of her life and legacy.

My brothers were always a raucous, hard-drinking, unpredictable gang of fox-hunting hounders, ranging across our lands at Roxborough and beyond in pursuit of those poor foxes and whatever else pleased them. I liked it that way, at least most times. (Although I've always enjoyed Oscar Wilde's definition of fox hunting: 'The unspeakable in pursuit of the uneatable'.) When my pious mother would lecture them about keeping the Sabbath, she graced them with her sing-song instruction:

This is the Sunday Sabbath Day;
This is why we must not play.

In sharing their rebellious response with each other, letting me overhear, they would whisper:

This is the Sunday Sabbath night;
This is why we'll have a fight.

Not at all housebound like us girls, they were free to fly about and make mischief when they were young. When older, bigger mischief. It was as if my sisters and I were there to enable all that but not participate in it. They were handsome, wild, broke all the rules, and had all the fun. I often wanted to *be* one of them.

There were sixteen of us in all, three by my father's first marriage, thirteen with my mother. I was the ninth of the thirteen. When my older brothers got old enough that illness set in, I was the still single little sister called upon to look after them. My glamorous trip to the Riviera in the winter of 1878–9 was as nursemaid to my very sick brother Richard. After he died and my eldest half-brother, Dudley, succeeded him as master of Roxborough, he fell ill shortly himself, and I was again a captive handmaiden.

Much later, after my beloved husband, William, had passed away, I returned to Roxborough with my son Robert, then eleven years old. My brother William was by that time presiding over Roxborough, usually drunkenly. He was a paranoid drunk, convincing himself that I wanted to displace him as lord of the manor. On a frigid New Year's Eve in 1892, in high drunken dudgeon, he ordered me to leave the house and never darken its doorstep again. I returned to Coole Park with Robert, its next master, in the darkest of despairing moods.

I felt homeless. Inauspiciously cast out of my own family's house, I limped back to the one I had shared with my husband. But now it belonged to my young son. I was his trustee, responsible to care for the place until he came of age. I remembered that my mother had had to leave Roxborough for a much more modest townhouse on Merrion Square in Dublin when Dudley inherited the property. Women in the Ireland of my time were not legal property-holding persons. Nor were they literary persons, by and large. The laws of landownership and of literature were men's preserves.

At one and the same time quietly rebelling against men and admiring their freedom and authority, I wanted to redefine myself beyond the dutiful daughter, sister and grieving young widow. In many ways, some I did not realise at the time, my relationships with William Gregory, Wilfrid Scawen Blunt, William Butler Yeats and John Quinn were all undertakings in the service of creating that new self. Over time I grew convinced that if I could manage the Coole Park estate, cultivating it for my son while using it to reposition myself in the process, I could work with and through them and other men to remake Irish literature and culture. I could create a home for myself in my country's contentious history that could never be discounted. The land becomes the literature, and both become the lady, shall we say?!

'Land' and 'war' are two words inextricably linked in that history. Perhaps that is part of why my sense of homelessness when Robert and I were dismissed from Roxborough was so profoundly disorienting and frightful. That feeling of violent displacement and loss haunted me full force again when Roxborough was destroyed in 1922. It had been occupied earlier by an armed group opposed to the Irish Free State government. Government forces drove them out, but the speculation was that some such group returned to pillage and burn the place. It somehow seemed inevitable that the oldest, deepest vestige of my old Anglo-Irish life would go up in smoke, as did so many of the grand houses.

My efforts to make Coole Park into a vanguard of a new multi-ethnic, multi-religious Irish life spared it that fate. But much later the political and business types in control of that new Irish life tore it down for the value of its stones. Still, much later again the Irish Republic made Coole Park into a sort of national monument, now part of the Irish National Parks and Wildlife Service. So some justice was finally done to the place.

More so when Mary Robinson, the first female President of Ireland, who had been elected as a redoubtable champion of women's rights, presided at the 8 August 1996 opening of the Kiltartan Gregory Museum, minutes down the Galway-to-Limerick road from Coole. I could have kissed her. I think I would have done if I had been there. The museum building is a special structure, the restored National School founded by my husband Sir William in 1892. The National Schools were meant to bring Catholic and Protestant students together in a non-proselytising educational environment. William worked with my brother Francis, an architect, to design a unique space with ornamental features that echo those found in Ceylon, where he had been Governor. I am thrilled that the Gregory family legacy is now embodied in a place whose face was 'ecumenical', embracing even South Asian influence.

The best thing about this opening day was that my two granddaughters, Anne and Nu, were the stars. Both by then old women themselves, they got to walk the Coole grounds once again and see images of themselves as wee girls with their brother, Richard, and their doting grandmother. Living in Devon, England, a few years before she died, Anne said that she often thought of those years at Coole, that she could always see that wonderful clear light of Galway. The Coole Park Visitor Centre and Tearooms are located in the converted barn and stables, of all places. I had certainly never swept out the stables when I presided as the lady at Coole, but now feel as though I have been – ceremoniously – swept into them for posterity. I wonder if the air for the visitors might not be so clear as the light Anne remembered!

Seeing Catherine and Anne so happy at the event triggered the memory of a bizarre chapter in Anne's life right out of the darker side of the Gregory family saga. It was a foreboding, rainy day in winter 1947 in Pola, a town then in Italy, later in Yugoslavia. The Allied supreme commander in the area, British Brigadier Robert de Winton, was to turn over the power from Italy to the Yugoslav authorities, as provided in the Paris peace treaties ending World War II. As he stepped out of his car for the ceremonial review of the troops preceding the transfer, a young woman in a red coat stepped forward from the small crowd gathered for the event. She fired three shots into his back, killing him instantly.

Maria Pasquinelli was an Italian fascist who bitterly opposed ceding the territory, which had been in Italian hands since the collapse of the Austro-Hungarian Empire at the end of World War I. She had denounced the murders of Italian civilians by Yugoslav Communist partisans. She wanted to assassinate the official who represented the authority she believed had countenanced that slaughter, and was about to reward it. That official, Robert de Winton, happened to be Anne's husband.

They had been married for only two years. She had joined Robert in Pola in January 1947 with their two-month-old son. A month later he was dead. Pasquinelli spent seventeen years in an Italian prison for the killing, but was then pardoned by the Italian government. Unrepentant, she lived to be one hundred years old.

I cannot but see the tragic parallels. I lost my son, Robert, in Italy in World War I at age thirty-six. That left Anne fatherless at the age of six. She lost her husband, Robert, in Italy in World War II at age thirty-eight. Both died in service to England, sucked into a war on a Continent that could never keep itself at peace for very long. Ethnic and religious hatreds there simmered always, and exploded into uncontainable violence periodically. As in Ireland, where both had their family connections, tribal loyalties easily perverted by chest-thumping men drove everything toward death and despair. Anne's full name was Augusta Anne Gregory. She shared too much of my sorrow and entanglement with all that. Like me, Anne lived a long life, with sixty-two years as a widow until her death at ninety-seven. We Gregory women have a knack for defying and surviving the vainglories of men and the ravenous empires they spawn to satisfy their egos.

The old myths, folklore, sagas and ballads I read so diligently and rewrote for modern Ireland have no one man's ego at their source, no owner-author. Rather, they are products of community memory and constant oral embellishment. The ghosts of voices past sing in them. They are spawned by people imagining together, and they bring people together in a common – in the best sense of that word – cultural enterprise. In them the 'I' fades into the 'we'. In that 'we' a national culture can be formed that transcends politics and its harsher brother, war. I brought powerful male egos to the table of that project and kept them there to help make the Irish Literary Renaissance.

I believe I was capable of that because in my own way I admired their single-minded drive and self-absorption, fed off it perhaps. I had been closely tutored in it as a young woman by my brothers, by my husband, by Wilfrid Blunt. I absorbed some of that heady self-absorption. How else could I have turned it outward to manage the sprawling estate and busy household at Coole Park, shape the contentious theatre companies that led to the Abbey Theatre, direct the Abbey's business as well as artistic affairs, and in addition to the plays I wrote and translations I undertook, produce all the diaries, journals, memoirs and other autobiographical writings that projected my voice and my own narrative out into the world during my life and after my death?

Women were not supposed to do that in my time, you know. There was always a terrible tension about it for me. This is how I explained what I was doing in my translation of the saga of the great Irish warrior-hero, Cuchulain. I dedicated it to the people of Kiltartan, for it was their community property from the Irish language that I was giving back to them in the English they now spoke:

> I have told the whole story in plain and simple words, in the same way my old nurse Mary Sheridan used to be telling stories from the Irish long ago, and I a child at Roxborough.
>
> And indeed if there was more respect for Irish things among the learned men that live in the college at Dublin, where so many of these old writings are stored, this work would not have been left to a woman of the house, that has to be minding the place, and listening to complaints, and dividing her share of food.

I was translating from Irish to English for the native Irish. I was stepping down to be one of them, to ghostwrite my dear Irish Catholic, Irish-speaking nurse in her rhythms and simplicity. I was a woman complaining about being distracted from my womanly household obligations at Coole to do manly things.

Yet those domestic responsibilities were really those of the lord of the manor. And the supposedly manly activities of carrying and transmitting a culture's understanding of itself, its values, are in fact often left to women, who largely raise the next generation. I knew I was blurring these already crooked lines of identity, and therefore the tension I felt.

But of course, none of us is fully one thing or another. As I have said, I have seemed to myself to be more sets of two things than most, especially when it comes to the feminine/masculine, Irish/English divide. It could be that feeling is rooted in my quarrel with my mother's insistence that in a world set right, all the Irish should be one thing – Anglo-Irish Protestants, all sharing an idealistic loyalty to the Crown and an aversion to Popery. That was why she was so reluctant when I suggested that Wilfrid Blunt would like to visit Roxborough. She had never had a Catholic under her roof before. Indeed, she had devoted herself without success to evangelising the local Catholics, under their own thatched roofs, into her brand of Church of England Protestantism.

When she finally relented and received Blunt at the house, she went on and on at him, poor man, about Jesuit intrigues, the hocus pocus of Catholic ritual, and as Chaucer would have it, shitten shepherds and clean flocks. My mother was an Irish religionist of the type so well characterised by George Bernard Shaw:

> Irish Protestantism was not then a religion: it was a side in political faction, a class prejudice, a conviction that Roman Catholics are socially inferior persons who will go to Hell when they die and leave Heaven in the exclusive possession of Protestant ladies and gentlemen.

Her pre-ordained banishment of Blunt from her Protestant pearly-gated Heaven made me love him even more in reaction and moved me to feel I was all in with him and with his ardent Irish nationalism.

Except for my unshakably English husband Sir William, all four of the men who caught and held my eye were nationalists – the Egyptian rebel Arabi Bey, and Blunt, Yeats and Quinn, each an Irish nationalist in his own unique fashion. I became a committed, sometimes militant comrade in cultural arms with those three men in ways I never imagined I could as a young woman at Roxborough and in my early years at Coole Park. Pulsing ceaselessly under my settled aristocratic surface was a desire to throw off the established order, in nation states and in romance. At first it was a secret, restless, rebellious streak, bred from resentment of the Roxborough family regime. Then it came to be writ large in politics and personal relationships. This in a woman who in her earlier years had tremulously kissed the Queen's hand and humbly received the Pope's personal blessing.

I developed my own understanding of politics and religion in England and Ireland that complemented Shaw's. Like him, I felt it in my bones, and I distilled it in my work. As I once wrote:

> To the English peasant the well-furnished village church, the pulpit cushion, the gilt-edged Bible, the cosy rectory represent respectability, comfort, peace, a settled life. In Ireland the peasant has always before his eyes, on his own cottage walls or in his white-washed chapel, the cross, the spear, the crown of thorns, that tell of what once seemed earthly failure, that tell that He to whom he kneels was led to a felon's death.

I will confess that there were times when I inclined sympathetically toward this latter Irish theology, at the farthest angle away from my mother's. Between 1915 and 1918 I could write no plays, consumed as I was with the crosses, spears and crowns of thorns of World War I, coming unsparingly home to my own 'cottage walls' with Robert's death. Again, between 1922 and 1923, the horrible time of all the brotherly bloodletting of the Irish civil conflict, I wrote nothing for the stage. Between these two periods, during the Anglo-Irish War, I took up a different pen.

I suppose I turned into a kind of polemicist against the utterly heedless violence that the British Black and Tans and the Auxiliaries inflicted upon Irish civilians, women and children included. I could not stand idly by. I sent by my standards almost lurid excerpts from my diary about their beastly behaviour to the nationalist *Nation* magazine in London. The *Nation* was happy to publish them as a series of 'A Week in Ireland' pieces, anonymously at my request. I did not want my family or myself to become a target.

One of the most egregious and heartbreaking outrages involved the pregnant wife of my former tenant, Malachy Quinn. Eileen Quinn, twenty-four years old, was doing nothing more than standing in front of her house in Gort one day in November 1920 with her three young children beside her. A lorry full of Black and Tans pulled up and simply opened fire. Eileen and her unborn baby died eight hours later. The British authorities declared it a case of 'death by misadventure' due to necessary 'precautionary shots'.

The local people believed it was revenge for the deadly ambush by the IRA two days earlier of a Royal Irish Constabulary officer, Constable Horan, himself the father of three. Reprisals against the local population in response to guerrilla attacks on Crown forces had become commonplace. Days after Eileen's killing, the Loughnane brothers, Pat and Harry, IRA members, were taken from their home by the RIC and Auxiliaries. They were tied to the back of a truck, dragged along the road, mutilated, burned, and then their bodies dumped into a muddy pond. I had to help turn British public opinion against this savagery, perpetrated in their name in Ireland.

The man who oversaw this policy of civilian terror was John French, or more properly, John Denton Pinkstone French, Viscount French, First Earl of Ypres. French had been commander of the British Expeditionary Force in World War I. When he was appointed Lord Lieutenant of Ireland in 1918, he seemed to believe that the bludgeoning tactics used on the Continent would work to subdue rebellion in Ireland. His analysis of the Irish situation boiled down to a regret that there were too many of us, especially younger ones, living here. He wrote in 1920: 'The principal cause of the trouble is the national stoppage of emigration for the last five years. There are here 100,000 to 200,000 young people who normally would have expatriated themselves'. Perhaps a twentieth-century version of the Great Famine of the mid-nineteenth would be timely in reducing the Irish population to a suitably weak level, removing by death and 'self-expatriation' large portions of the current and future generations.

The pathetic irony here is that French, although born in Kent, was from an Anglo-Irish family and always considered himself an Irishman. His father was from the branch of the Frenches of Frenchpark in County Roscommon. In 1917 John French himself had bought a country house at Drumdoe in Frenchpark. He even purchased a second one, Hollypark, near Boyle in Roscommon in 1920. With monumental lack of judgement, he thought he could have a happy, peaceful, Irish Ascendancy retirement between the two. But the disdain of the Irish for the cruelty he had unleashed upon Ireland as Lord Lieutenant – and for him personally – made that country retirement far too uncomfortable. In a calculated insult, the Republicans looted much of the furniture from Drumdoe during the Irish Civil War. So in a twisted sense he 'self-expatriated' after short stays at both houses. We were well done with him.

I have to admit that I am embarrassed by the likes of French, by, shall I say, the density, the lack of self-awareness, of the Protestant Ascendancy in Ireland generally. Too many seemed to think they rightly owned their peculiar brand of Irishness without having earned a whit of it. After Sean O'Casey, a poor Protestant from the Dublin slums, a far remove indeed from the Ascendancy, came out to visit Coole, he wrote of my two chief loves: books 'nearest her mind' and trees 'nearest her heart'. Well, the books are made from the trees after all. I laboured to grow a new Irish identity and culture from the land up, from the folk memories of those who worked the land. The weakness and instability of so many other Anglo-Irish landlords was that while their families held questionable title to the land, as did we, they were never attached to it as I was. Whether absentee or resident, they took profit and ease for themselves from it, not communal sustenance.

In the great copper beech tree at Coole, the 'autograph' tree, creators who drew from the soil of Ireland with my encouragement – the likes of Yeats, his brother Jack, Synge, Edward Martyn, George Moore, Douglas Hyde and O'Casey – carved themselves back into it. At the 1898 centenary of the United Irishmen rebellion, one led in the northeast by Irish Presbyterians chafing under the yoke imposed by their establishment Anglican brethren, I made a suggestion based on the idea that a conscious, shared gesture at improving the Irish landscape might symbolise our mutual Irishness. I recommended that every nationalist should plant at least one tree in Irish ground in 1898, and every unionist in 1900, and every waverer or indifferent person in the intervening year.

With Coole Park now a national reserve, a public park in its own right, people from Ireland and all over the world can enjoy the trees I planted there. Its woods and wetlands are open to all. They can stroll its trails, hear its birds, see and smell the great variety of its plants, and encounter some of its wild animals. The house is gone, but the stable yard, some old stone walls, and a limekiln remain. Best of all, Coole Lake is still there. Or should I say there and gone and back again?

Coole Lake is a turlough, from the Irish 'tuar' meaning dry, and of course 'lough' meaning lake – a dry lake, a contradiction in terms rather like being Anglo-Irish. The lake empties in the summer through 'swallow holes' in its lakebed, cracks in the karstic limestone. The water makes its way from Coole northwest via an alternating series of other turloughs and underground pathways to reach the Atlantic finally at Kinvara. The lake level will fluctuate more in Coole Lake than in any other turlough in Ireland – in excess of ten metres, refilling itself for the winter. These kinds of seasonal lakes are found in Ireland more commonly than in any other place in the world.

It was my favourite place at Coole Park. It seems to me a natural model of what I wanted Coole to be. My home would summon from across Ireland the best thinking and writing about its past, present and future. From there it would flow back out across the Irish landscape and on to the rest of the world. Gradually, the world's reaction to it would refill and reshape our own Irish creative energies, with us now as players on the big world's cultural stage, with the world wondering how this divided little island, floating out in the daunting Atlantic Ocean, could have produced such marvels.

I am delighted that I and the other ghosts who have spoken here can see that now. It is the most glorious form of immortality. I once wrote to Wilfrid Blunt, as I could have to the people who became these other ghosts: 'I believe we shall meet again after death […] but if we don't you will have the worst of it, for you can't say anything to me, and if we do, I will say, "I told you so"'. I rest in peace in no small part because I believe I got the best of it for Ireland from each of them.

Sources

The sources I used in developing each of the book's chapters are listed under the respective chapter numbers. In the initial section below, I cite sources that helped shape my views more generally of the genres of life writing, and of the Ireland and the world in which the chapter speakers lived.

The citations under Chapters 1 and 10, in both of which the ghost of Lady Gregory is the speaker, are sources that relate most directly to her life. Because she is the main character in the book, these sources certainly inform all the chapters. In particular, the influences of Lady Gregory's own writings and two excellent, full-length biographies of her are reflected in all the chapters. Those biographies are Judith Hill's *Lady Gregory: An Irish Life* (Stroud, Gloucestershire: Sutton, 2005) and Mary Lou Kohfeldt's *Lady Gregory: The Woman Behind the Irish Renaissance* (New York: Atheneum, 1985).

Printed Sources
General Background

Bradley, Anthony, and Maryann Gialanella Valiulis, eds, *Gender and Sexuality in Modern Ireland* (Amherst, MA: University of Massachusetts Press, 1997).

Cusack, George, *The Politics of Identity in Irish Drama: W. B. Yeats, Augusta Gregory and J. M. Synge* (New York: Routledge, 2009).

Darin, Doris, *Sean O'Casey* (New York: Frederick Ungar, 1976).

Frazier, Adrian, *Behind the Scenes: Yeats, Horniman, and the Struggle for the Abbey Theatre* (Berkeley: University of California Press, 1990).

Fryer, Paul, ed., *Women and the Arts in the Belle Epoque: Essays on Influential Artists, Writers and Performers* (Jefferson, NC: McFarland, 2012).

Garner, Dwight, 'In Dublin, a Book Critic Finds Literary Ghosts', *New York Times* (16 October 2024).

Greene, David H., and Edward M. Stephens, *J. M. Synge, 1871–1909* (New York: New York University Press, 1989).

Gregory, Vere R. T., *The House of Gregory* (Dublin: Browne and Nolan, 1943).

Grene, Nicholas, *The Politics of Irish Drama: Plays in Context from Boucicoult to Friel* (Cambridge: Cambridge University Press, 1999).

Grubgeld, Elizabeth, *Anglo-Irish Autobiography: Class, Gender, and the Forms of Narrative* (Syracuse: Syracuse University Press, 2004).

Harte, Liam, ed., *A History of Irish Autobiography* (Cambridge: Cambridge University Press, 2018).

----, *Modern Irish Autobiography: Self, Nation and Society* (New York: Palgrave Macmillan, 2007).

Levitas, Ben, *The Theatre of Nation: Irish Drama and Cultural Nationalism 1890–1916* (Oxford: Clarendon Press, 2002).

Lynch, Claire, *Irish Autobiography: Stories of Self in the Narrative of a Nation* (Bern: Peter Lang, 2009).

McGarry, Fearghal, *The Abbey Rebels of 1916: A Lost Revolution* (Dublin: Gill & Macmillan, 2015).

Napier, Taura S., *Seeking a Country: Literary Autobiographies of Twentieth-Century Irishwomen* (Lanham, MD: Rowman & Littlefield, 2001).

O'Connor, Joseph, *Ghost Light* (London: Harvill Secker, 2010).

Reilly, Kevin P., 'Irish Literary Autobiography: The Goddesses That Poets Dream Of', *Eire-Ireland* xvi/3 (1981), 57–80.

Richards, Shaun, ed., *The Cambridge Companion to Twentieth Century Irish Drama* (Cambridge: Cambridge University Press, 2004).

Rogers, James Silas, *Irish-American Autobiography: The Divided Hearts of Athletes, Priests, Pilgrims, and More* (Washington, D.C.: The Catholic University of America Press, 2017).

Steele, Karen, *Women, Press and Politics During the Irish Revival* (Syracuse: Syracuse University Press, 2007).

Trotter, Mary, *Ireland's National Theaters: Political Performance and the Origins of the Irish Dramatic Movement* (Syracuse: Syracuse University Press, 2001).

Preface

Yeats, W. B., *The Collected Poems of W. B. Yeats* (New York: Macmillan, 1956).

Chapters 1 and 10: Lady Augusta Gregory Ave and Lady Augusta Gregory Vale

Coxhead, Elizabeth, *Lady Gregory: A Literary Portrait* (London: Secker and Warburg, 1966).

Gregory, Anne, *Me and Nu: Childhood at Coole* (Gerrards Cross, Buckinghamshire: Colin Smythe Ltd, 1970).

Gregory, Augusta, *Coole*, ed., Colin Smythe from the MS. (Dublin: Dolmen Press, 1971).

―――, *Cuchulain of Muirthemne: The Story of the Men of the Red Branch of Ulster* (New York: Oxford University Press, 1973).

―――, *Lady Gregory's Diaries, 1892–1902*, ed., James Pethica (Gerrards Cross, Buckinghamshire: Colin Smythe Ltd, 1996).

―――, *Lady Gregory's Journals*, vol. 2, ed., Daniel J. Murphy (Oxford: Oxford University Press, 1988).

―――, *Lady Gregory's Journals, 1916–1930*, ed., Lennox Robinson (New York: Putnam, 1946).

―――, *Our Irish Theatre: A Chapter of Autobiography* (Gerrards Cross, Buckinghamshire: Colin Smythe Ltd, 1972).

―――, *Selected Plays* (Gerrards Cross, Buckinghamshire: Colin Smythe Ltd, 1975).

―――, *Selected Writings*, eds., Lucy McDiarmid and Maureen Waters (London: Penguin Books, 1995).

―――, *Seventy Years: Being the Autobiography of Lady Gregory* (Gerrards Cross, Buckinghamshire: Colin Smythe Ltd, 1973).

―――, *Visions and Beliefs in the West of Ireland* (New York: Putnam, 1920).

Hill, Judith, *Lady Gregory: An Irish Life* (Stroud, Gloucestershire: Sutton Publishing, 2005).

Kohfeldt, Mary Lou, *Lady Gregory: The Woman Behind the Irish Renaissance* (New York: Atheneum, 1985).

Kopper, Edward A., Jr, *Lady Isabella Persse Gregory* (Boston: Twayne, 1976).

Mikhail, E. H., ed., *Lady Gregory: Interviews and Recollections* (Lanham, MD: Rowman & Littlefield, 1977).

Pearse, Patrick, *The Literary Writings of Patrick Pearse*, ed., Seamus O Buachalla (Dublin and Cork: The Mercier Press, 1979).

Saddlemyer, Ann, and Colin Smythe, eds., *Lady Gregory, Fifty Years After* (Gerrards Cross, Buckinghamshire: Colin Smythe Ltd, 1987).

Saddlemyer, Ann, ed., *Theatre Business, The Correspondence of the First Abbey Directors: William Butler Years, Lady Gregory and J. M. Synge* (University Park, Pennsylvania State University, 1982).

Smythe, Colin, *A Guide to Coole Park, Home of Lady Gregory* (Gerrards Cross, Buckinghamshire: Colin Smythe Ltd, 1995).

Tóibín, Colm, *Lady Gregory's Toothbrush* (Madison: University of Wisconsin Press, 2002).

Chapter 2: Sir William Gregory

Gregory, Augusta, ed., *Sir William Gregory, K. C. M. G., Formerly Member of Parliament and Sometime Governor of Ceylon: An Autobiography* (London: J. Murray, 1894).

Jenkins, Brian, *Sir William Gregory of Coole: The Biography of an Anglo-Irishman* (Gerrards Cross, Buckinghamshire: Colin Smythe Ltd, 1986).

Chapter 3: Wilfrid Scawen Blunt

Blunt, Wilfrid Scawen, *The Land War in Ireland: Being a Personal Narrative of Events* (London: Stephen Swift, 1912).

----, *My Diaries: Being a Personal Narrative of Events, 1888–1914, Part One, (1888–1900)* (New York: Knopf, 1922).

Longford, Elizabeth, *A Pilgrimage of Passion* (New York: Knopf, 1980).

Chapter 4: John Quinn

Gregory, Augusta, *The Letters of Lady Gregory to John Quinn*, ed., Daniel Joseph Murphy (Ann Arbor: University Microfilms, 1981).

Quinn, John, *The Letters of John Quinn to William Butler Yeats*, ed.. Alan Himber (Ann Arbor: UMI Press, 1983).

Reid, B. L., *The Man from New York: John Quinn and His Friends* (New York: Oxford University Press, 1968).

Chapter 5: William Butler Yeats

Foster, R. F., *W. B. Yeats, A Life* (Oxford: Oxford University Press, Vols 1 and 2, 2004).

Gwynn, Stephen, ed., *Scattering Branches: Tributes to the Memory of W. B. Yeats* (New York: Macmillan, 1940).

Maddox, Brenda, *Yeats's Ghosts: The Secret Life of W. B. Yeats* (New York: HarperCollins, 1999).

Yeats, W. B., *Autobiographies* (London: Macmillan, 1955).

----, *The Collected Letters of W. B. Yeats*, ed. John Kelly (Oxford: Clarendon Press, 1986).

----, *The Collected Plays of W. B. Yeats* (New York: Macmillan, 1953).

----, *The Collected Poems of W. B. Yeats* (New York: Macmillan, 1956).

Chapter 6: Maud Gonne

Bendheim, Kim, *The Fascination of What's Difficult: A Life of Maud Gonne* (New York: OR Books, 2021).

The Editors, *'Who We Are in Irish Studies'*, Interview with Caoimhe Nic Dhaibheid, Irish Literary Supplement (Fall 2024).

Ferguson, Trish, *Maud Gonne* (Dublin: University College Dublin Press, 2019).

Frazier, Adrian, *The Adulterous Muse: Maud Gonne, Lucien MIllevoye and W. B. Yeats* (Dublin: The Lilliput Press, 2016).

Gonne, Iseult, *Letters to W. B. Yeats and Ezra Pound from Iseult Gonne*, eds., A. Norman Jeffares, Anna MacBride White and Christina Bridgwater (New York: Palgrave Macmillan, 2004).

Gonne, Maud, *The Autobiography of Maud Gonne: A Servant of the Queen*, eds., A. Norman Jeffares and Anna MacBride White (Chicago: University of Chicago Press, 1995).

-----, *Maud Gonne's Irish Nationalist Writings, 1895–1946*, ed. by Karen Steele (Portland, OR: Irish Academic Press, 2004).

Londraville, Janis and Richard, eds., *Too Long a Sacrifice: The Letters of Maud Gonne and John Quinn* (Cranbury, NJ: Associated University Presses, 1999).

MacBride, Sean, *That Day's Struggle: A Memoir, 1904–1951*, ed., Caitriona Lawlor (Blackrock: Currach Press, 2005).

Ward, Margaret, *Maud Gonne: Ireland's Joan of Arc* (London: Pandora Press, 1990).

-----, *Unmanageable Revolutionaries: Women and Irish Nationalism, 1880–1980* (Dublin: Arlen House, 2021).

Chapter 7: Hugh Lane

Gregory, Augusta, *Hugh Lane's Life and Achievement, with Some Account of the Dublin Galleries* (London: John Murray, 1921).

O'Byrne, Robert, *Hugh Lane, 1875–1915* (Dublin: Lilliput Press, 2018).

Chapter 8: Maire Nic Shiubhlaigh

Nic Shiubhlaigh, Maire, *The Splendid Years: The Memoirs of an Abbey Actress and 1916 Rebel*, ed. David Kenny (Stillorgan: New Island Books, 2016).

Chapter 9: Robert Gregory

Anonymous, 'Ballyturin (Ballyturn) Ambush', Irelandxo, <https://www.irelandxo.com>, accessed 25 October 2024.

Anonymous, 'Ballyturin (or Ballyturn) Ambush, Gort, Galway', The Auxiliaries, <https://www.the auxiliaries.com>, accessed 25 October 2024.

McGreevy, Ronan, "Those That I Fight I Do Not Hate' – An Irishman's Diary on Robert Gregory', *The Irish Times* (23 January 2018).

Quinlan, Ailin, 'A Diary Has Revealed the Playwright's Shock at Her Son's Love Affair, Despite an Illicit Relationship of Her Own, Writes Peggy Cronin', *The Independent* (27 December 2021).

Smith, Adrian, 'Major Robert Gregory, and the Irish Air Aces of 1917–18', *20th-century/Contemporary History, Features*, 9/4 (2001).

Archival Sources

Gregory Family Papers, Stuart A. Rose Manuscript, Archives, and Rare Book Library, Emory University.

Lady Gregory Papers, Berg Collection, The New York Public Library.

John Quinn Papers, Manuscripts and Archives Division, The New York Public Library.

Reimagining Ireland

Series Editor: Dr Eamon Maher, Technological University Dublin

The concepts of Ireland and 'Irishness' are in constant flux in the wake of an everincreasing reappraisal of the notion of cultural and national specificity in
a world assailed from all angles by the forces of globalisation and uniformity. Reimagining Ireland interrogates Ireland's past and present and suggests possibilities
for the future by looking at Ireland's literature, culture and history and subjecting them to the most up-to-date critical appraisals associated with sociology, literary theory, historiography, political science and theology.

Some of the pertinent issues include, but are not confined to, Irish writing in English and Irish, Nationalism, Unionism, the Northern 'Troubles', the Peace Process,
economic development in Ireland, the impact and decline of the Celtic Tiger, Irish spirituality, the rise and fall of organised religion, the visual arts, popular cultures, sport, Irish music and dance, emigration and the Irish diaspora, immigration and multiculturalism, marginalisation, globalisation, modernity/postmodernity and postcolonialism. The series publishes monographs, comparative studies, interdisciplinary projects, conference proceedings and edited books.

Proposals should be sent either to Dr Eamon Maher at eamon.maher@ittdublin.ie
or to ireland@peterlang.com.

Vol. 1	Eugene O'Brien: 'Kicking Bishop Brennan up the Arse': Negotiating Texts and Contexts in Contemporary Irish Studies ISBN 978-3-03911-539-6. 219 pages. 2009.
Vol. 2	James P.Byrne, Padraig Kirwan and Michael O'Sullivan (eds): Affecting Irishness: Negotiating Cultural Identity Within and Beyond the Nation ISBN 978-3-03911-830-4. 334 pages. 2009.
Vol. 3	Irene Lucchitti: The Islandman: The Hidden Life of Tomás O'Crohan ISBN 978-3-03911-837-3. 232 pages. 2009.
Vol. 4	Paddy Lyons and Alison O'Malley-Younger (eds): No Country for Old Men: Fresh Perspectives on Irish Literature ISBN 978-3-03911-841-0. 289 pages. 2009.
Vol. 5	Eamon Maher (ed.): Cultural Perspectives on Globalisation and Ireland ISBN 978-3-03911-851-9. 256 pages. 2009.
Vol. 6	Lynn Brunet: 'A Course of Severe and Arduous Trials': Bacon, Beckett and Spurious Freemasonry in Early Twentieth-Century Ireland ISBN 978-3-03911-854-0. 218 pages. 2009.
Vol. 7	Claire Lynch: Irish Autobiography: Stories of Self in the Narrative of a Nation ISBN 978-3-03911-856-4. 234 pages. 2009.

Vol. 8	Victoria O'Brien: A History of Irish Ballet from 1927 to 1963 ISBN 978-3-03911-873-1. 208 pages. 2011.
Vol. 9	Irene Gilsenan Nordin and Elin Holmsten (eds): Liminal Borderlands in Irish Literature and Culture ISBN 978-3-03911-859-5. 208 pages. 2009.
Vol. 10	Claire Nally: Envisioning Ireland: W. B. Yeats's Occult Nationalism ISBN 978-3-03911-882-3. 320 pages. 2010.
Vol. 11	Raita Merivirta: The Gun and Irish Politics: Examining National History in Neil Jordan's Michael Collins ISBN 978-3-03911-888-5. 202 pages. 2009.
Vol. 12	John Strachan and Alison O'Malley-Younger (eds): Ireland: Revolution and Evolution ISBN 978-3-03911-881-6. 248 pages. 2010.
Vol. 13	Barbara Hughes: Between Literature and History: The Diaries and Memoirs of Mary Leadbeater and Dorothea Herbert ISBN 978-3-03911-889-2. 255 pages. 2010.
Vol. 14	Edwina Keown and Carol Taaffe (eds): Irish Modernism: Origins, Contexts, Publics ISBN 978-3-03911-894-6. 256 pages. 2010.
Vol. 15	John Walsh: Contests and Contexts: The Irish Language and Ireland's Socio-Economic Development ISBN 978-3-03911-914-1. 492 pages. 2011.
Vol. 16	Zélie Asava: The Black Irish Onscreen: Representing Black and Mixed-Race Identities on Irish Film and Television ISBN 978-3-0343-0839-7. 213 pages. 2013.
Vol. 17	Susan Cahill and Eóin Flannery (eds): This Side of Brightness: Essays on the Fiction of Colum McCann ISBN 978-3-03911-935-6. 189 pages. 2012.
Vol. 18	Brian Arkins: The Thought of W. B. Yeats ISBN 978-3-03911-939-4. 204 pages. 2010.
Vol. 19	Maureen O'Connor: The Female and the Species: The Animal in Irish Women's Writing ISBN 978-3-03911-959-2. 203 pages. 2010.
Vol. 20	Rhona Trench: Bloody Living: The Loss of Selfhood in the Plays of Marina Carr ISBN 978-3-03911-964-6. 327 pages. 2010.
Vol. 21	Jeannine Woods: Visions of Empire and Other Imaginings: Cinema, Ireland and India, 1910–1962 ISBN 978-3-03911-974-5. 230 pages. 2011.

Vol. 22	Neil O'Boyle: New Vocabularies, Old Ideas: Culture, Irishness and the Advertising Industry ISBN 978-3-03911-978-3. 233 pages. 2011.
Vol. 23	Dermot McCarthy: John McGahern and the Art of Memory ISBN 978-3-0343-0100-8. 344 pages. 2010.
Vol. 24	Francesca Benatti, Sean Ryder and Justin Tonra (eds): Thomas Moore: Texts, Contexts, Hypertexts ISBN 978-3-0343-0900-4. 220 pages. 2013.
Vol. 25	Sarah O'Connor: No Man's Land: Irish Women and the Cultural Present ISBN 978-3-0343-0111-4. 230 pages. 2011.
Vol. 26	Caroline Magennis: Sons of Ulster: Masculinities in the Contemporary Northern Irish Novel ISBN 978-3-0343-0110-7. 192 pages. 2010.
Vol. 27	Dawn Duncan: Irish Myth, Lore and Legend on Film ISBN 978-3-0343-0140-4. 181 pages. 2013.
Vol. 28	Eamon Maher and Catherine Maignant (eds): Franco-Irish Connections in Space and Time: Peregrinations and Ruminations ISBN 978-3-0343-0870-0. 295 pages. 2012.
Vol. 29	Holly Maples: Culture War: Conflict, Commemoration and the Contemporary Abbey Theatre ISBN 978-3-0343-0137-4. 294 pages. 2011.
Vol. 30	Maureen O'Connor (ed.): Back to the Future of Irish Studies: Festschrift for Tadhg Foley ISBN 978-3-0343-0141-1. 359 pages. 2010.
Vol. 31	Eva Urban: Community Politics and the Peace Process in Contemporary Northern Irish Drama ISBN 978-3-0343-0143-5. 303 pages. 2011.
Vol. 32	Mairéad Conneely: Between Two Shores/*Idir Dhá Chladach*: Writing the Aran Islands, 1890–1980 ISBN 978-3-0343-0144-2. 299 pages. 2011.
Vol. 33	Gerald Morgan and Gavin Hughes (eds): Southern Ireland and the Liberation of France: New Perspectives ISBN 978-3-0343-0190-9. 250 pages. 2011.
Vol. 34	Anne MacCarthy: Definitions of Irishness in the 'Library of Ireland' Literary Anthologies ISBN 978-3-0343-0194-7. 271 pages. 2012.
Vol. 35	*Forthcoming.*

Vol. 36   Eamon Maher and Eugene O'Brien (eds): Breaking the
          Mould: Literary Representations of Irish Catholicism
          ISBN 978-3-0343-0232-6. 249 pages. 2011.

Vol. 37   Mícheál Ó hAodha and John O'Callaghan (eds): Narratives of the Occluded Irish
          Diaspora: Subversive Voices
          ISBN 978-3-0343-0248-7. 227 pages. 2012.

Vol. 38   Willy Maley and Alison O'Malley-Younger (eds): Celtic
          Connections: Irish–Scottish Relations and the Politics of Culture
          ISBN 978-3-0343-0214-2. 247 pages. 2013.

Vol. 39   Sabine Egger and John McDonagh (eds): Polish–Irish Encounters in
          the Old and New Europe
          ISBN 978-3-0343-0253-1. 322 pages. 2011.

Vol. 40   Elke D'hoker, Raphaël Ingelbien and Hedwig Schwall (eds): Irish
          Women Writers: New Critical Perspectives
          ISBN 978-3-0343-0249-4. 318 pages. 2011.

Vol. 41   Peter James Harris: From Stage to Page: Critical Reception of Irish
          Plays in the London Theatre, 1925–1996
          ISBN 978-3-0343-0266-1. 311 pages. 2011.

Vol. 42   Hedda Friberg-Harnesk, Gerald Porter and Joakim Wrethed
          (eds): Beyond Ireland: Encounters Across Cultures
          ISBN 978-3-0343-0270-8. 342 pages. 2011.

Vol. 43   Irene Gilsenan Nordin and Carmen Zamorano Llena (eds): Urban
          and Rural Landscapes in Modern Ireland: Language, Literature and Culture
          ISBN 978-3-0343-0279-1. 238 pages. 2012.

Vol. 44   Kathleen Costello-Sullivan: Mother/Country: Politics of the Personal
          in the Fiction of Colm Tóibín
          ISBN 978-3-0343-0753-6. 247 pages. 2012.

Vol. 45   Lesley Lelourec and Gráinne O'Keeffe-Vigneron (eds): Ireland and Victims:
          Confronting the Past, Forging the Future
          ISBN 978-3-0343-0792-5. 331 pages. 2012.

Vol. 46   Gerald Dawe, Darryl Jones and Nora Pelizzari (eds): Beautiful
          Strangers: Ireland and the World of the 1950s
          ISBN 978-3-0343-0801-4. 207 pages. 2013.

Vol. 47   Yvonne O'Keeffe and Claudia Reese (eds): New Voices, Inherited
          Lines: Literary and Cultural Representations of the Irish Family
          ISBN 978-3-0343-0799-4. 238 pages. 2013.

Vol. 48   Justin Carville (ed.): Visualizing Dublin: Visual Culture, Modernity
          and the Representation of Urban Space
          ISBN 978-3-0343-0802-1. 326 pages. 2014.

| Vol. 49 | Gerald Power and Ondřej Pilný (eds): Ireland and the Czech Lands: Contacts and Comparisons in History and Culture
ISBN 978-3-0343-1701-6. 243 pages. 2014. |
|---|---|
| Vol. 50 | Eoghan Smith: John Banville: Art and Authenticity
ISBN 978-3-0343-0852-6. 199 pages. 2014. |
| Vol. 51 | María Elena Jaime de Pablos and Mary Pierse (eds): George Moore and the Quirks of Human Nature
ISBN 978-3-0343-1752-8. 283 pages. 2014. |
| Vol. 52 | Aidan O'Malley and Eve Patten (eds): Ireland, West to East: Irish Cultural Connections with Central and Eastern Europe
ISBN 978-3-0343-0913-4. 307 pages. 2014. |
| Vol. 53 | Ruben Moi, Brynhildur Boyce and Charles I. Armstrong (eds): The Crossings of Art in Ireland
ISBN 978-3-0343-0983-7. 319 pages. 2014. |
| Vol. 54 | Sylvie Mikowski (ed.): Ireland and Popular Culture
ISBN 978-3-0343-1717-7. 257 pages. 2014. |
| Vol. 55 | Benjamin Keatinge and Mary Pierse (eds): France and Ireland in the Public Imagination
ISBN 978-3-0343-1747-4. 279 pages. 2014. |
| Vol. 56 | Raymond Mullen, Adam Bargroff and Jennifer Mullen (eds): John McGahern: Critical Essays
ISBN 978-3-0343-1755-9. 253 pages. 2014. |
| Vol. 57 | Máirtín Mac Con Iomaire and Eamon Maher (eds): 'Tickling the Palate': Gastronomy in Irish Literature and Culture
ISBN 978-3-0343-1769-6. 253 pages. 2014. |
| Vol. 58 | Heidi Hansson and James H. Murphy (eds): Fictions of the Irish Land War
ISBN 978-3-0343-0999-8. 237 pages. 2014. |
| Vol. 59 | Fiona McCann: A Poetics of Dissensus: Confronting Violence in Contemporary Prose Writing from the North of Ireland
ISBN 978-3-0343-0979-0. 238 pages. 2014. |
| Vol. 60 | Marguérite Corporaal, Christopher Cusack, Lindsay Janssen and Ruud van den Beuken (eds): Global Legacies of the Great Irish Famine: Transnational and Interdisciplinary Perspectives
ISBN 978-3-0343-0903-5. 357 pages. 2014. |
| Vol. 61 | Katarzyna Ojrzyn'ska: 'Dancing As If Language No Longer Existed': Dance in Contemporary Irish Drama
ISBN 978-3-0343-1813-6. 318 pages. 2015. |

Vol. 62	Whitney Standlee: 'Power to Observe': Irish Women Novelists in Britain, 1890–1916 ISBN 978-3-0343-1837-2. 288 pages. 2015.
Vol. 63	Elke D'hoker and Stephanie Eggermont (eds): The Irish Short Story: Traditions and Trends ISBN 978-3-0343-1753-5. 330 pages. 2015.
Vol. 64	Radvan Markus: Echoes of the Rebellion: The Year 1798 in Twentieth-Century Irish Fiction and Drama ISBN 978-3-0343-1832-7. 248 pages. 2015.
Vol. 65	B. Mairéad Pratschke: Visions of Ireland: Gael Linn's Amharc Éireann Film Series, 1956–1964 ISBN 978-3-0343-1872-3. 301 pages. 2015.
Vol. 66	Una Hunt and Mary Pierse (eds): France and Ireland: Notes and Narratives ISBN 978-3-0343-1914-0. 272 pages. 2015.
Vol. 67	John Lynch and Katherina Dodou (eds): The Leaving of Ireland: Migration and Belonging in Irish Literature and Film ISBN 978-3-0343-1896-9. 313 pages. 2015.
Vol. 68	Anne Goarzin (ed.): New Critical Perspectives on Franco-Irish Relations ISBN 978-3-0343-1781-8. 271 pages. 2015.
Vol. 69	Michel Brunet, Fabienne Gaspari and Mary Pierse (eds): George Moore's Paris and His Ongoing French Connections ISBN 978-3-0343-1973-7. 279 pages. 2015.
Vol. 70	Carine Berbéri and Martine Pelletier (eds): Ireland: Authority and Crisis ISBN 978-3-0343-1939-3. 296 pages. 2015.
Vol. 71	David Doolin: Transnational Revolutionaries: The Fenian Invasion of Canada, 1866 ISBN 978-3-0343-1922-5. 348 pages. 2016.
Vol. 72	Terry Phillips: Irish Literature and the First World War: Culture, Identity and Memory ISBN 978-3-0343-1969-0. 297 pages. 2015.
Vol. 73	Carmen Zamorano Llena and Billy Gray (eds): Authority and Wisdom in the New Ireland: Studies in Literature and Culture ISBN 978-3-0343-1833-4. 263 pages. 2016.
Vol. 74	Flore Coulouma (ed.): New Perspectives on Irish TV Series: Identity and Nostalgia on the Small Screen ISBN 978-3-0343-1977-5. 222 pages. 2016.
Vol. 75	Fergal Lenehan: Stereotypes, Ideology and Foreign Correspondents: German Media Representations of Ireland, 1946–2010 ISBN 978-3-0343-2222-5. 306 pages. 2016.

| Vol. 76 | Jarlath Killeen and Valeria Cavalli (eds): 'Inspiring a Mysterious Terror': 200 Years of Joseph Sheridan Le Fanu
ISBN 978-3-0343-2223-2. 260 pages. 2016. |

| Vol. 77 | Anne Karhio: 'Slight Return': Paul Muldoon's Poetics of Place
ISBN 978-3-0343-1986-7. 272 pages. 2017. |

| Vol. 78 | Margaret Eaton: Frank Confessions: Performance in the Life-Writings of Frank McCourt
ISBN 978-1-906165-61-1. 294 pages. 2017. |

| Vol. 79 | Marguérite Corporaal, Christopher Cusack and Ruud van den Beuken (eds): Irish Studies and the Dynamics of Memory: Transitions and Transformations
ISBN 978-3-0343-2236-2. 360 pages. 2017. |

| Vol. 80 | Conor Caldwell and Eamon Byers (eds): New Crops, Old Fields: Reimagining Irish Folklore
ISBN 978-3-0343-1912-6. 200 pages. 2017. |

| Vol. 81 | Sinéad Wall: Irish Diasporic Narratives in Argentina: A Reconsideration of Home, Identity and Belonging
ISBN 978-1-906165-66-6. 282 pages. 2017. |

| Vol. 82 | Ute Anna Mittermaier: Images of Spain in Irish Literature, 1922–1975
ISBN 978-3-0343-1993-5. 386 pages. 2017. |

| Vol. 83 | Lauren Clark: Consuming Irish Children: Advertising and the Art of Independence, 1860–1921
ISBN 978-3-0343-1989-8. 288 pages. 2017. |

| Vol. 84 | Lisa FitzGerald: Re-Place: Irish Theatre Environments
ISBN 978-1-78707-359-3. 222 pages. 2017. |

| Vol. 85 | Joseph Greenwood: 'Hear My Song': Irish Theatre and Popular Song in the 1950s and 1960s
ISBN 978-3-0343-1915-7. 320 pages. 2017. |

| Vol. 86 | Nils Beese: Writing Slums: Dublin, Dirt and Literature
ISBN 978-1-78707-959-5. 250 pages. 2018. |

| Vol. 87 | Barry Houlihan (ed.): Navigating Ireland's Theatre Archive: Theory, Practice, Performance
ISBN 978-1-78707-372-2. 306 pages. 2019. |

| Vol. 88 | María Elena Jaime de Pablos (ed.): Giving Shape to the Moment: The Art of Mary O'Donnell: Poet, Novelist and Short Story Writer
ISBN 978-1-78874-403-4. 228 pages. 2018. |

| Vol. 89 | Marguérite Corporaal and Peter Gray (eds): The Great Irish Famine and Social Class: Conflicts, Responsibilities, Representations
ISBN 978-1-78874-166-8. 330 pages. 2019. |

Vol. 90	Patrick Speight: Irish-Argentine Identity in an Age of Political Challenge and Change, 1875–1983 ISBN 978-1-78874-417-1. 360 pages. 2020.
Vol. 91	Fionna Barber, Heidi Hansson, and Sara Dybris McQuaid (eds): Ireland and the North ISBN 978-1-78874-289-4. 338 pages. 2019.
Vol. 92	Ruth Sheehy: The Life and Work of Richard King: Religion, Nationalism and Modernism ISBN 978-1-78707-246-6. 482 pages. 2019.
Vol. 93	Brian Lucey, Eamon Maher and Eugene O'Brien (eds): Recalling the Celtic Tiger ISBN 978-1-78997-286-3. 386 pages. 2019.
Vol. 94	Melania Terrazas Gallego (ed.): Trauma and Identity in Contemporary Irish Culture ISBN 978-1-78997-557-4. 302 pages. 2020.
Vol. 95	Patricia Medcalf: Advertising the Black Stuff in Ireland 1959–1999: Increments of Change ISBN 978-1-78997-345-7. 218 pages. 2020.
Vol. 96	Anne Goarzin and Maria Parsons (eds): New Cartographies, Nomadic Methologies: Contemporary Arts, Culture and Politics in Ireland ISBN 978-1-78874-651-9. 204 pages. 2020.
Vol. 97	Hiroko Ikeda and Kazuo Yokouchi (eds): Irish Literature in the British Context and Beyond: New Perspectives from Kyoto ISBN 978-1-78997-566-6. 250 pages. 2020.
Vol. 98	Catherine Nealy Judd: Travel Narratives of the Irish Famine: Politics, Tourism, and Scandal, 1845–1853 ISBN 978-1-80079-084-1. 468 pages. 2020.
Vol. 99	Lesley Lelourec and Gráinne O'Keeffe-Vigneron (eds): Northern Ireland after the Good Friday Agreement: Building a Shared Future from a Troubled Past? ISBN 978-1-78997-746-2. 262 pages. 2021.
Vol. 100	Eamon Maher and Eugene O'Brien (eds): Reimagining Irish Studies for the Twenty-First Century ISBN 978-1-80079-191-6. 384 pages. 2021.
Vol. 101	Nathalie Sebbane: Memorialising the Magdalene Laundries: From Story to History ISBN 978-1-78707-589-4. 334 pages. 2021.
Vol. 102	Roz Goldie: A Dangerous Pursuit: The Anti-Sectarian Work of Counteract ISBN 978-1-80079-187-9. 268 pages. 2021.
Vol. 103	Ann Wilson: The Picture Postcard: A New Window into Edwardian Ireland ISBN 978-1-78874-079-1. 282 pages. 2021.

Vol. 104	Anna Charczun: Irish Lesbian Writing Across Time: A New Framework for Rethinking Love Between Women ISBN 978-1-78997-864-3. 320 pages. 2022.
Vol. 105	Olivier Coquelin, Brigitte Bastiat and Frank Healy (eds): Northern Ireland: Challenges of Peace and Reconciliation Since the Good Friday Agreement ISBN 978-1-78997-817-9. 298 pages. 2022.
Vol. 106	Jo Murphy-Lawless and Laury Oaks (eds): The Salley Gardens: Women, Sex, and Motherhood in Ireland ISBN 978-1-80079-417-7. 338 pages. 2022.
Vol. 107	Mercedes del Campo: Voices from the Margins: Gender and the Everyday in Women's Pre- and Post-Agreement Troubles Short Fiction ISBN 978-1-78874-330-3. 324 pages. 2022.
Vol. 108	Sean McGraw and Jonathan Tiernan: The Politics of Irish Primary Education: Reform in an Era of Secularisation ISBN 978-1-80079-709-3. 532 pages. 2022.
Vol. 109	Gerald Dawe: Northern Windows/Southern Stars: Selected Early Essays 1983–1994 ISBN 978-1-80079-652-2. 180 pages. 2022.
Vol. 110	John Fanning: The Mandarin, the Musician and the Mage: T. K. Whitaker, Seán Ó Riada, Thomas Kinsella and the Lessons of Ireland's Mid-Twentieth-Century Revival ISBN 978-1-80079-599-0. 296 pages. 2022.
Vol. 111	Gerald Dawe: Dreaming of Home: Seven Irish Writers ISBN 978-1-80079-655-3. 108 pages. 2022.
Vol. 112	John Walsh: One Hundred Years of Irish Language Policy, 1922–2022 ISBN 978-1-78997-892-6. 394 pages. 2022.
Vol. 113	Bertrand Cardin: Neil Jordan, Author and Screenwriter: The Imagination of Transgression ISBN 978-1-80079-923-3. 286 pages. 2023.
Vol. 114	David Clark: Dark Green: Irish Crime Fiction 1665–2000 ISBN 978-1-80079-826-7. 450 pages. 2022.
Vol. 115	Aida Rosende-Pérez and Rubén Jarazo-Álvarez (eds): The Cultural Politics of In/Difference: Irish Texts and Contexts ISBN 978-1-80079-727-7. 274 pages. 2022.
Vol. 116	Tara McConnell: "Honest Claret": The Social Meaning of Georgian Ireland's Favourite Wine ISBN 978-1-80079-790-1. 346 pages. 2022.

Vol. 117   M. Teresa Caneda-Cabrera (ed.): Telling Truths: Evelyn Conlon and the Task of Writing
ISBN 978-1-80079-481-8. 228 pages. 2023.

Vol. 118   Alexandra Maclennan (ed.): The Irish Catholic Diaspora: Five Centuries of Global Presence
ISBN 978-1-80079-516-7. 264 pages. 2023.

Vol. 119   Brian J. Murphy: Beyond Sustenance: An Exploration of Food and Drink Culture in Ireland
ISBN 978-1-80079-956-1. 328 pages. 2023.

Vol. 120   Fintan Cullen (ed.): Ireland and the British Empire: Essays on Art and Visuality
ISBN 978-1-78874-299-3. 264 pages. 2023.

Vol. 121   Natalie Wynn and Zuleika Rodgers (eds): Reimagining the Jews of Ireland: Historiography, Identity and Representation
ISBN 978-1-80079-083-4. 308 pages. 2023.

Vol. 122   Paul Butler: A Deep Well of Want: Visualising the World of John McGahern
ISBN 978-1-80079-810-6. 244 pages. 2023.

Vol. 123   Carlos Menéndez Otero: The Great Pretenders: Genre, Form, and Style in the Film Musicals of John Carney
ISBN 978-1-80374-135-2. 258 pages. 2023.

Vol. 124   Gerald Dawe: Politic Words: Writing Women | Writing History
ISBN 978-1-80374-259-5. 208 pages. 2023.

Vol. 125   Marjan Shokouhi: From Landscapes to Cityscapes: Towards a Poetics of Dwelling in Modern Irish Verse
ISBN 978-1-80079-870-0. 260 pages. 2023.

Vol. 126   Pat O'Connor: A 'proper' woman? One woman's story of success and failure in academia
ISBN 978-1-80374-305-9. 248 pages. 2023.

Vol. 127   Natalie Wynn: Community, Identity, Conflict: The Jewish Experience in Ireland, 1881–1914
ISBN 978-1-78707-483-5. 338 pages. 2024.

Vol. 128   Marie-Violaine Louvet: The Irish Against the War: Post-Colonial Identity & Political Activism in Contemporary Ireland
ISBN 978-1-80079-998-1. 296 pages. 2024.

Vol. 129   Anne Rainey: Hiberno-English, Ulster Scots and Belfast Banter: Ciaran Carson's Translations of Dante and Rimbaud
ISBN 978-1-80374-070-6. 338 pages. 2024.

Vol. 130   Nicole Volmering, Claire M. Dunne, John Walsh and Noel Ó Murchadha (eds): Irish in Outlook: A Hundred Years of Irish Education
ISBN 978-1-80374-090-4. 348 pages. 2024.

| Vol. 131 | Grace Neville, Sarah Nolan and Eugene O'Brien (eds): 'Getting the Words Right': A Festschrift in Honour of Eamon Maher
ISBN 978-1-80374-144-4. 382 pages. 2024. |
|---|---|
| Vol. 132 | Hiroko Ikeda: Sweeney's Revival: Translating and transcending the liminal
ISBN 978-1-80374-429-2. 192 pages. 2024. |
| Vol. 133 | Maria Gaviña-Costero, Dina Pedro, and Dónall Mac Cathmhaoill (eds): 'Lost, Unhappy and at Home': The Impact of Violence on Irish Culture: Volume I: Literature
ISBN 978-1-80374-321-9. 296 pages. 2024. |
| Vol. 134 | Maria Gaviña-Costero, Dina Pedro, and Dónall Mac Cathmhaoill (eds): 'Lost, Unhappy and at Home': The Impact of Violence on Irish Culture: Volume II: Socio-Cultural Aspects
ISBN 978-1-80374-318-9. 312 pages. 2024. |
| Vol. 135 | Graham Spencer: The SDLP, Politics and Peace: The Mark Durkan Interviews
ISBN 978-1-80079-940-0. 288 pages. 2025. |
| Vol. 136 | Seán William Gannon and Natalie Wynn (eds): The Limerick Boycott in Context
ISBN 978-1-80079-899-1. 320 pages. 2025. |
| Vol. 137 | Connal Parr and Stephen Hopkins (eds): Paving the Path to Peace: Civil Society and the Northern Ireland Peace Process
ISBN 978-1-80374-332-5. 332 pages. 2025. |
| Vol. 138 | Germán Asensio Peral, Madalina Armie, Verónica Membrive (eds): A Nation, not A Parish: The Homewhere-s and Elsewhere-s of 1930s Irish Culture
ISBN 978-1-80374-848-1. 298 pages. 2025. |
| Vol. 139 | Tom Inglis: Unbecoming Catholic: Being Religious in Contemporary Ireland
ISBN 978-1-80374-817-7. 212 pages. 2025. |
| Vol. 140 | Conor Curran: Blue Chippers from the Emerald Isle: A history of Irish footballers and scholarships in the USA in the twentieth century
ISBN 978-1-80374-739-2. 328 pages. 2025. |
| Vol. 141 | Flore Coulouma, Cornelius Crowley and Florence Schneider (eds): Strange Country: Ireland's Politics and Culture, 1998-2021
ISBN 978-1-80374-601-2. 332 pages. 2025. |
| Vol. 142 | Eamonn Wall: Conocimiento: Writing Irish Borderlands
ISBN 978-1-80374-870-2. 214 pages. 2025. |
| Vol. 143 | Ian Kennedy: Prime the Pump: Catholic Social Teaching, Arts Policy and the Post-war Irish Amateur Drama Movement 1949 to 1969
ISBN 978-1-80374-598-5. 350 pages. 2025. |
| Vol. 144 | Seán Creagh: Republican Solipsist: The Life and Times of Joseph McGarrity, 1874–1940
ISBN 978-1-80374-893-1. 270 pages. 2025. |

Vol. 145	Geoffrey Sloan: Seeking Success and Confronting Failure. The British Army's campaigns in Ireland and Northern Ireland 1919-2007 ISBN 978-1-80374-816-0. 276 pages. 2025.
Vol. 146	James McAuley, Graham Spencer and Máire Braniff: A Companion to Conflict and Peace in Northern Ireland ISBN 978-1-80079-867-0. 588 pages. 2025.
Vol. 147	Kevin P. Reilly: Gregory Ghosts: Haunting Irishness ISBN 978-1-80374-742-2. 154 pages. 2026.

www.peterlang.com

www.ingramcontent.com/pod-product-compliance
Ingram Content Group UK Ltd.
Pitfield, Milton Keynes, MK11 3LW, UK
UKHW022226230426
12048UKWH00016BA/1079